The
New Breed
of
Clergy

The
New Breed
of
Clergy

CHARLES PRESTWOOD

WILLIAM B. EERDMANS PUBLISHING COMPANY
Grand Rapids, Michigan

Preface

I consider myself a member of the new breed of clergy. The heights of modern scholarship have thrilled me; the restlessness of menial jobs has bored me; the pangs of poverty have haunted me; the insensitivity of the Establishment has frightened me; the excitement of the civil rights movement has grasped me; role conflicts have threatened me; and finally, external tension has forced me to seek a new means of earning my bread at middle age. I taught for several years at a small state college in the deep South and am now teaching at a small, church-related liberal arts college in Pennsylvania. During the ten years before I started teaching, I attended church renewal meetings, civil rights meetings, and political rallies. I preached in black churches both large and small; I addressed striking teachers; and I baited politicians in high places. Since I went to the front of the high school auditorium serving as a sanctuary for a church without a place to worship in order to give my life to God, I have had only two ambitions, one of which was to be a Methodist preacher. Today I spend most of my time teaching young minds sociology, but I still consider myself a Methodist preacher. As I look back, I feel only a sense of thanksgiving for the privilege of being a part of the Church in these days. I have been pastor of four different churches in Alabama and western Florida. While

I was serving one church in the black belt of Alabama, the press announced that I had been appointed to serve on the Alabama Advisory Committee to the U. S. Commission on Civil Rights. In another, I saw Negroes seated at worship amidst the tension of the Selma March. In another, a Negro came to preach in our church for the first time in the history of the city. As I reflect upon these events in these hours, I am still amazed that in the Church I found support and love from some great laymen. I believe in the Church, and I believe in the new breed of clergy.

This book is written in an attempt to explain to laymen, the Establishment, fellow clergy, and perhaps to many friends among the new breed something of our dreams, frustrations, thought, and soul. I am no official spokesman for the new breed; in fact, many among the new breed would even question my right to speak about them. I feel, however, that the time has come for someone who has shared some of their dreams, hurts, and humiliations to say something about the new breed. The materials included in this text in a small way reflect traditional academic research, but the book is not intended to be a contribution to that subtle world of scholarship which is removed from the deep passions that affect judgment. I hope that I have said nothing that will prove to be embarrassing to the profession in which I am now engaged, teaching. To me this text is both a confession and a prayer.

The ideas, feelings, and actions reflected in this manuscript grow out of having been a minister in the churches of the deep South during the ten years in which a revolution took place both in the South and in the churches. They grow out of the long nights I have spent with ministers, young and old, who were searching in a world coming apart for a means of making their witness in their time to their Lord. They grow out of secret meetings with white and black clergy in a mutual quest for an island of sanity in a sea of insanity. Reflected in these pages are the joys of being a member of the Alabama Advisory Committee to the U. S. Civil Rights Commission from 1959 to 1965, a time in which we moved from secret meetings in out-of-the-way places to the Civil Rights Acts of 1960, 1964, 1965, and 1968.

The emotions recorded here range from the hurt inflicted by unknown voices cursing over the phone in the early hours of the morning to the pleasure of joining hands with five hundred students at midnight on the Morris Brown College campus, singing, "We Shall Overcome." Erupting across these pages is the memory of friends beaten to death in the streets of Selma and slain on a balcony in Memphis. But most conspicuous in my mind is a group of ministers who left universities, logging camps, law offices, and lives of quiet desperation to join in a common effort to bring the gospel of Jesus to bear on a world that at times has refused to listen. The ministers who hover around me as I write come from all sections of the country and from all denominations. While our fathers were attending august meetings in great hotels in the hope of bringing an ecumenical spirit, we found that spirit in the parlors of small churches, in the lobbies of cheap hotels, and in the streets of America.

In these years, I saw the raw courage which only those who have a dream can know. I saw boys become men and priests become prophets. When I think of them, I feel like one of Thomas Wolfe's characters whom he describes as "being cursed with the passion, but never blessed with the power." This book is written in homage to my friends whom some have come to call "the new breed of clergy."

Some of them will read it in a quiet church study, but others, I know, will have to read it between classes at some small school or amidst the bustle of some Headstart program or back on some lonely farm. Many of them have been casualties in the war of nerves and will perhaps be unable to read it. At least three are dead, and I may never be able to tell them what a joy their lives brought to all of us. This book is a prayer that the Church will open its mind and its heart to those whom I know to be among the chosen.

–C.P.

Contents

1

The Ministry Is Many

The Christian Church is an almost infinite variety of people, theology, ritual, rubric, and organization. Their unity is not found in a common polity, universal creed, or a shared sense of mission. The unity of the Church is found in its Lord. In the Church is found not only a variety of gifts, but also a variety of interests, understandings, and traditions. As the Church is one, it is also many—and so it seems always to have been.

The claim of Catholic Pope and Quaker friend to be the legitimate heirs of faith "once delivered to the saints" are both saved from the preposterous only by the clear recognition that the memory of the New Testament Church is not preserved for us in a cognitive package devoid of poetry, imagery, and symbolism. The record of the New Testament Church was written by excited men who had shared a vision in which there was glory, sorrow, hope, and salvation. Their tools were not those of quantitative sociology or linguistic analysis, but rather those of poetry, symbolism, and analogy, expressions of minds seared by an experience rather than tutored by historiography.

The Church is one, and yet it is many. The ministry of the Church too is one, yet it is many. Bishop, deacon,

elder, exhorter, teacher, healer, prophet, and priest are all
found in the New Testament tradition. (Let it be noted,
however, that the New Testament knows of no office
called executive secretary or district superintendent.)

The office of the minister is not now, nor has it ever
been, simply a textual and a theological question. The
office of the minister has from the day of the early
Church been surrounded with necessary questions of
funding, role expectancies, and the existential needs of
people, which were not only theological but also social
and political. St. Paul reflects in his letters the ambivalence of the early Church concerning the role of the
minister, the funding of the ministry, and the authority
of the ministry. The greatest minds of the Church have
been able to resolve these questions for only a part of the
Church, and only for brief periods. Men at various times,
under various circumstances, from various socioeconomic
classes, and with various abilities, needs, and freedoms
have sought a church after their own heart; and the result
has been constant tension in the Church concerning the
minister's office, role, authority, and means of funding.
Perhaps the real genius of the Church is in its remarkable
flexibility as much as in its message. The ability of the
Church to proclaim the gospel among the rich and the
poor, among the free and the captive, in the East and the
West is in no small measure due to the flexibility of form
which some wrongly call the shame of denominational-
ism.

In a day when the variety of forms among the churches
and their ministry is perceived to be part of our sin,
perhaps it will startle ecumenists to consider the possibility that diversity of form may emanate from God rather
than from demonic man. The emergence of an ecumenical church with a social action orientation in the

West must be praised. The willingness and ability of the
Church to become a voice for those who have no voice
seems to be a legitimate fulfillment of the mission of the
Church. However, it should be recognized that the role of
the Church in the open, democratic society of the West is
possible in part because of the economic, social, and
political atmosphere in which it finds itself. The right of
the Church to speak openly today concerning questions
of foreign and domestic policy is protected in the consti-
tutions, mores, and traditions which the voice of the
Church helped to create. But the Church does not always
find itself in such conditions. The freedom of a specific
church to indulge in advocacy roles in the political de-
bates of a nation may be seriously circumscribed by the
type of government and tradition surrounding it. There
are forms of ministry for the Church which are meaningful in the context of Western democracy but impossible
in nations where Christianity is a minority movement and
where the state has taken firm steps to curtail and eliminate the Church. The Church may find itself always in an
alien culture, but it finds itself in some cultures, such as
England and the United States, in which the alienation is
benign and in other cultures, such as China and Russia,
where the alienation is belligerent. The Church has seldom held the power to dictate the social and political
context in which it finds itself. The ability of the Church
to adopt many different forms of ministry and polity, to
fund its ministers in a variety of ways, keeps the proclamation of the gospel a live option in a variety of sociopolitical contexts. It is not total foolishness to believe
that the ability of the Church in Russia to adopt new
forms after the Revolution may have saved us all from
extinction, for it was willing to be an invisible fellowship
when by action of the state it could no longer be the

visible cathedral. The Church and its clergy cannot create
the world in which they *choose* to find themselves. They
can only proclaim the gospel in the world in which they
do find themselves, with the full assurance that God is in
all things working for good.

As the Church finds itself in a variety of sociopolitical
contexts, it also faces a variety of foes. The sin of man
remains a constant fact in the history of man, but its
manifestations and institutional forms are legion. The
Church cannot determine what its competition will be
and what form it will take. In the South there is a saying
which has significant insight concerning a certain type of
minister: "He fights the Devil where he used to be."
There are forms of the Church that are more valuable in
meeting some threats than are other forms. Indeed there
are times when the form of the Church is itself an enemy
to the faith. There have been threats to the Church that
demanded tight discipline within it; on the other hand,
there have been other times when the cause of the gospel
seemed best served by an open, experimental form. There
are circumstances in which the foes of the Church can
best be met with the beauty and grandeur of liturgy and
studied homily, and there are times when the foes of the
Church can be met by personal, folksy talks in the parlors
of worn cottages or in the plain surroundings of a con-
verted shop. Discipline to ensure the purity of the gospel
and freedom to preach it unashamedly are needed by the
Church and the clergy at different times and often in
different forms. The loose cooperation and ordination
policies that made possible the spread of scriptural holi-
ness across the frontier of the New World are inadequate
to meet the nascent racism present in America during the
last decades of the twentieth century. And the Church
will discover that firm pronouncements from a united

ecumenical voice, so necessary in attacking racism, will be inadequate to deal with the fears of people who are fleeing in great numbers to the drug culture and the counterculture. The existential demands of history may preempt the possibility of certain forms of ministry, but they cannot preempt the possibility of witness to the faith or the fact that people are led to believe the witness when they hear it.

Ancient sages said rightly that man is a social animal. Modern social science has taught us that man is a cultural animal, ever developing language, norms, ideas, artifacts, and life styles to meet his real and perceived needs. Before most Americans were able to accept the fact that there were social classes with profound differences in our land, social science moved to a serious and as yet unresolved debate concerning the existence of a culture of poverty. Because we are now aware of the subjective nature of language, we cannot assume that unity of creed and firmness of canon would provide a common faith even if we were united in profession of faith and form. The Church cannot determine by proclamation alone what is heard! Nor can the Church create a classless society in which all persons will perceive its message in the same way. For if the Church tries to proclaim the gospel in the same manner for all people, it will thereby exclude large numbers of people from hearing its message.

Uniformity of form, language, and polity does not make the Church one; it simply makes it incurably middle class. The emergence of the Pentecostal movement, not only in America but also in England, Sweden, Africa, and Russia, is ample testimony that even where the established Church chooses to be one, history still makes the Church many.

Further, the established Church and its ministry are not the only cup God uses for the outpouring of his Spirit. The Church should not lament this crucial fact as the failure of the Church and its ministry, but should rejoice that God is forever at work beyond the consciousness and ability of the Church. The Kingdom of God works in ways as unanticipated by the Church as they are unmanageable. For all of its wisdom the Church could not have planned the beauty of a St. Francis in its Prayer Life Commission, the Wesleyan revival in its Department of Evangelism, or the civil rights revolution in America in its Board of Christian Social Concerns. Things happen which upon reflection cause the Christian to rejoice but which he could never have anticipated.

The various branches of Christianity must ever be mindful of the waste involved in duplication and must courageously work with the others in love and good fellowship to proclaim the gospel. Where denominations cannot walk arm in arm, they must walk hand in hand. Yet the fact that the Church and its ministry are many is not to be despised but to be praised.

Let us now look at the unity of the ministry which transcends the ever-changing variety of its temporary forms. The minister is compelled to proclaim the Word faithfully and to testify to what he has seen and heard of God's acts in human experience. This unity of the ministry is not found in comity or polity. It is found in at least four salient features of the faith: in a series of historical events; in the collective experience of the Church; in a living, dynamic faith within a constantly changing world; and in the constant redemptive presence of God in Christ reconciling the world unto himself.

The ministry is called into being by the fact that Jesus

did live, was crucified, and is raised for the Church in the resurrection experience. Wherever one opens his mouth to testify, he shares this fact with all its power and meaning. It stands as the source of our unity and as a judge upon our acts of proclamation. God acting in Christ was not granting congregational franchises but was calling man to obedience.

The unity of the ministry is found in the collective experience of the community of faith. The redemptive message of God was delivered not to one person but to a community of faith which was compelled to testify to the world and also to one another. The gospel as shared in the first century was a community experience. The gospel as recorded in the New Testament is a community memory and record. The minister is ever a member of a community of faith testifying about a faith delivered to a community, and in this testimony the unity of the ministry is manifest.

The gospel is not old business; it is constantly God's new business for the world. The New Testament is not a book which we pound to call the world to order for the minutes of a previous meeting; rather it is a message which we proclaim to call man to obedience. The gospel is a living, dynamic call in an ever-changing world. The minister as a part of the testimony of the Church is continually called to new forms of proclamation. The unity of the ministry is found in the living and dynamic experience of God in human history.

The redemptive presence of God in Christ reconciling the world unto himself is not the end of the New Testament message; it is the beginning. The New Testament and church history record case after case when the call of God came to men and movements both outside and inside the established Church. The persistence of God in redeeming men and movements for his purposes is a miracle that all ministers share. Ministers have authority because God is in Christ reconciling the world unto himself. Although ministers may not share the same polity or ordination, they share the common miracle of God's redemptive calling. Therein rests their unity.

Because the ministry is many and yet one, the Church must always be alert to what God is doing through it, lest it become hopelessly lost in its attempts to save and be saved. The secular age, the space age, the age of mass noncommunication, and the revolution of rising expectations have descended upon the Church poignantly in the past decade. On the surface the Church is torn between a thousand forces ranging from "concerned laymen" to Jesus freaks. For some, the only hope is to turn time back on the ecclesiastical clock and to cast the unmanageable problems to Satan. On the other hand, there are all too many churchmen and clergy who wait like vultures for the Church to fall in ruins before their eyes. In our hearts and heads, we know all too well that we shall neither turn time backwards nor see the Church fall into ruins in a takeover by young Turks.

Prayerfully we anticipate change in the Church, if it means a more faithful testimony to the faith. However, we have become painfully aware that change demands new awareness and new commitments.

The clergy are a major part, and a symbol, of the change taking place in the Church. It is my hope that we can look together at the ministry of the Church in an attempt to see some of the reasons for its haunting fears, diversities, and problems, perceiving at the same time its unity and hope for a community of faith which proclaims the redemptive message of God. Diversity among men committed to Christ does not necessarily lead to divisiveness. Unity among men bound in love does not necessarily mean uniformity.

2

The Changing Profession

The signs are clear that there is a pervasive difficulty within the Church that runs as deep and is becoming as disruptive as the Reformation in the Church of the sixteenth century. Despite the continued presence of the ecumenist, the Church is becoming increasingly a divided and racist institution. The more the Church talks of relevancy, the more irrelevant it becomes. Catholic orders are closing seminaries because there are few candidates for the priesthood. Protestant seminaries are able to hold their level of enrollment simply because they have dropped the standards of enrollment so low that they now take a pulse rather than academic, emotional, or moral achievement as an adequate basis for admission to the profession of the ministry. Every denomination is losing members and ministers. Even the Southern Baptists, who have traditionally used rescue mission theology and an American Legion social conscience to grow while others foolishly praised their evangelism, are in trouble. In 1968 they found that more Baptist ministers were leaving the ministry than a combination of all the informal methods of ordination could replace. The Roman Catholic Church is behaving as if some of the priests and the laymen have discovered that the "shoes of the fisher-

man" have been worn in a barnyard. The United Methodist Church has discovered that at least one major merger
per decade is necessary to offset the consistent loss of
membership. They have also discovered that ecumenism
works better when they merge into the most white of
white   denominations—the   former   German-speaking
denominations. The Episcopal Church has survived for
one hundred years by taking clergy from other denominations and teaching them the melodious habits that will
provide comfort for the affluent who are looking for a
new church in which to act out their newly found status.
It can hardly be denied that significant change needs to
be made in the Church, from the bureaucratic castles
around Riverside Drive in New York City to the un-
painted chapels of racism in rural Alabama. In spite of
these portents of trouble in the Church, it is still over-
whelmingly characterized as an institution doing the
traditional thing in a traditional manner; and it is surely
controlled by men who not only perform the traditional
roles but also consider the traditional role the right if not
the only role of the Church.

The clergy are the persons most directly affected by
the omnibus difficulty within the Church and by the
concentration of authority in the hands of the traditional, inflexible, and confused Establishment. The departure of men from the ministry is only one indication,
perhaps the least important, of what is happening to the
clergy. The rising rate of mental illness, heart attacks, and
psychosomatic disorders among clerics is another indication of what is happening to the ministry as a profession. The new religious experiences such as those ad-
vocated by the Glad Tidings Fellowship, the Lay Witness
movement, and the prayer groups are other symptoms of
the psychopathological religion which is a response of the

clergy to their situation. The difficulty of the ministry at present has obviously had a serious impact upon the profession, the individual ministers, the Church, and the persons to whom the Church attempts to minister. Samuel Blizzard has suggested, "The future of the Church may stand or fall on the mental health of the clergy."* The mental health of the clergyman may stand or fall on the understanding he has of his profession as the institutional Church goes through the terrors of a theological, psychological, sociological, and perhaps a political revolution. The following pages will be an attempt to look at the ministry as a profession, both from the factual perspective of the recent studies made of the profession and from the existential perspective of one who has been involved in and is perhaps a victim of the changes that relate to the profession.

*Samuel W. Blizzard, "Role Conflicts of the Urban Protestant Parish Minister," City Church, VII (Sept. 1956), 13, quoted in Richard D. Knudten, The Sociology of Religion (New York: Appleton-Century-Crofts, 1967), p. 217.

3

Specialization Versus Generalization

The Church, like any other institution, has developed a pattern of organization which is technically bureaucratic. Since the pioneer work of Weber, social scientists and administrators have not only recognized that institutions in a rational and legal society are bureaucracies but have also come to accept the value judgment that bureaucracies are the most efficient means to organize and administer institutions. Even though those who occupy positions of authority and prestige in the Church seem to resent the title "bureaucrat," they are nonetheless bureaucrats in one of the most bureaucratic of institutions—the Church.

At this point I am not concerned with the dysfunctional aspects of the bureaucracy but rather with that perennial characteristic of bureaucracy: specialization, both as a condition and as a norm. A cursory examination of the yellow pages of a telephone directory will reveal that the organization of the institutions in our society is highly specialized. Professions such as medicine, law, and architecture are listed by specialties. The clergy, on the other hand, when they are listed at all, are all listed together. In a society that is increasingly specialized, the Church as an institution should share in the trend toward specialization which is characteristic of bureaucracies.

Indeed, there is specialization in the institution of the Church. But it is located in the administration, beyond the local church. When it is found in the local church, it is such a rare commodity that people come from miles around to view the great curiosity. Denominations all have people in administrative positions who are specialists in finance, missions, audiovisual techniques, evangelism, prayer groups, social concerns, family devotions, counseling of unmarried mothers, discussion techniques, teaching, preaching, drama, art criticism, and leaf study. This specialization increases the pressure on the local minister to specialize, but he can usually do no more than feel guilty because he cannot conform to the norms of specialization. The institutional norms demand specialization; the clientele expect specialization; the minister desires specialization; but the local parish organization prohibits specialization. The demands for specialization and the impossibility of achieving it therefore create ambivalence within the ministry as a profession. After a study of the role of the clergy, Glock and Stark concluded that "both minister and parishioner are pleading for a greater specialization in a situation which inhibits specialization."*

The reasons for the lack of specialization in the parish ministry as a profession are various. No specialization is possible without funding which provides at least a living wage for the specialist. In the institutional Church this funding may come from one of three sources. A specialist

*Charles Y. Glock and Rodney Stark, *Religion and Society in Tension* (Chicago: Rand McNally, 1965), p. 150.

may charge his clientele fees sufficient to fund the role; he may raise funds from individuals who feel his specialization meets a need important enough to deserve their support, whether they use the specialized services or not; or the institution may fund his specialization. None of these sources seems to be sufficient in the case of the ministry.

With the exception of the evangelist, there are few roles of specialization for which the values of the profession include either a system of fees or a pattern of remuneration. Ministers who have attempted to charge for specialized services such as counseling have encountered significant resistance among their fellow clergy, their congregation, and, indeed, their clientele. The clientele of the ministry are no different from any other in that they will not pay for something they can get free somewhere else. In a study of the referral practices of clergy, Bentz has shown that ministers attempt to handle counseling problems themselves in direct relationship to the *absence* of training or education. Further, those among the better-trained ministers who do refer clients to agencies or other professions discover that there is almost no reverse referral.* With rare exceptions the sanction system, which makes charging for services difficult for the minister, the willingness of other ministers to perform the service *gratis,* and the fact that few agencies or other professionals refer persons to the minister add to the complication of funding a specialized ministerial role, with the exception of the evangelistic role, by charging the clientele.

---

*W. Kenneth Bentz, "The Relationship Between Educational Background and the Referral Role of Ministers," *Sociology and Social Research,* LI, 206.

If the minister attempts to fund his specialization by raising funds among persons and groups who feel that his specialization meets a real need, albeit not their own, he finds his support to be unpredictable. The fund-raising tactics adopted by many of the right-wing clergy for their anticommunist activities are simply incongruous with the professional standards held by most of the clergy with enough training to specialize.

The third means of funding specialization for the ministry is to have the role funded by the local church as an additional ministry or by the denomination as a special ministry. There are many reasons why these means are inadequate, but the most determinative one is that neither the local church nor the denomination has either the money or the real desire to redirect money for a specialized ministry.

Specialization is an elusive achievement in the Church partly because the local church, the clientele of the minister, has little appreciation for professional standards beyond the expectancy that the minister embody the ethics of pietism. The local church, according to an excellent study by Schroeder and Obenhaus, has little regard for biblical and theological scholarship or other indices by which one measures the professional preparation of the ministry. The congregation evaluates a minister primarily on the basis of "congeniality and good personality."*

Congeniality and good personality may be as good a way to evaluate a minister as any other. As long as these are the primary means by which a minister is evaluated, however, there seems to be substance to the claim that

*W. Widick Schroeder and Victor Obenhaus, *Religion in American Culture* (New York: Free Press, 1964), p. 240.

the ministry defies specialization. Thus we must recognize that the ministry remains a generalized profession in a society whose other professions are all moving toward specialization.

4

Role Expectancy: Church
Types and Sect Types

The tension in the minister's self-evaluation of his role
was not created by the Billy Grahams, the Martin Luther
Kings, the Bishop Pikes, or even the National Council of
Churches. The high visibility of role models such as these
only accentuated a trend that had been developing in the
traditional denominations for a generation, a trend which
led inevitably to mounting tension concerning the role of
the minister. Since the time of Ernst Troeltsch, students
of the Church have profitably analyzed it in the categories of "church type" and "sect type." Even though
the typology of Troeltsch has been significantly modified
by recent research, it remains a useful tool for an understanding of the role confusion of the clergy.

The church type of institution is oriented around a
sacramental concept of the ministry, whereas the sect
type is oriented around a charismatic ministry. The two
institutions demand radically different life styles of their
ministers. American churches have developed a church-
type image at the upper echelons of the denomination; at
the local church level, however, we still have a sect type
of institution. The minister evaluates his ministry to a

great extent from a church-type point of view, but the congregation evaluates him from a sect-type expectation. Scanzoni has concluded that the church-type church makes demands of a minister that are significantly different from those of a sect-type church. The sect-type clergy have a total work orientation in which they are expected to be available at all hours for numerous meetings and services and to minister to the personal needs that are related to immediate crises and family conflicts characteristic of their lower-middle-class parishioners.* The church-type clergy in a more sacramental institution tend to interpret the demands made upon them in a different perspective—a perspective that does not preclude immediate attention to domestic difficulties but simply does not always demand it.

When the clergy assume a church-type orientation but are judged by the congregation by sect-type standards, the inevitable result is role conflict. Thus, difference in evaluation creates tension over the place and time of the minister in his own family and over what, and how much, is expected of the minister.

The church-type and sect-type evaluations of the minister are also reflected in the other chief source of role confusion between the minister and the local congregation. The role of the clergyman is evaluated among his clientele, the local congregation, by what is visible in his professional activity. In the church-type concept of his role in which the minister operates, the professional activities that are most valuable in ascribing status—counseling and administration—are largely invisible to the

*John Scanzoni, "Resolution of Occupational-Conjugal Role Conflict in Clergy Marriages," *Journal of Marriage and Family*, XXVII, 401-2.

overwhelming majority of parishioners. On the other hand, the most disruptive activity from the view of ascribed status—social action—is the most visible activity to the average parishioner. Whether the individual minister is involved in social action or not, the entire profession is as affected by the high visibility of clergymen in civil rights demonstrations and peace demonstrations as it is by the high visibility of a Billy Graham. Thus the role of the ministry is complicated by the low visibility of such functions as counseling and administration and the high visibility of the activity of clergy in demonstrations and other social action projects. The traits of the church-type role that would have greatest ascribed status among the congregation are invisible, and those most disruptive are of highest visibility.

The mounting tension between the minister's self-evaluation of his role as church type and the congregation's perception of that role as sect type brings to the minister an impossible task of role consistency.

5

Role Models and Role Expectancy

If a group of scholars gathered to plan a means of creating a situation in which there would be maximum tension between self-role, role model, and role expectancy, they could devise no more effective structure than that which we find in the ministry today.

A minister develops his understanding of his role primarily by what he ideally considers his role to be and by how he feels others evaluate what they see of his role. In the ministry understanding of role is based on the ministers' professional training, the role models, the role expectancy of peer groups, and the role expectancy which is discovered (sometimes too late) in the congregation. There are aspects of each of these sources which contribute to role conflict, confusion, and discontinuity. They each have demands for time, standards, and life style which go beyond ambivalence to direct competition and conflict.

With rare exceptions, the seminaries in America are located in metropolitan areas and in many cases are directly or indirectly related to major universities. The urban community and the seminaries provide a variety of interest-creating and interest-consuming institutions. At least for the three years in seminary, the young minister is located "where the action is." The seminary student shares the general anonymity characteristic of the metropolitan community and the relatively high tolerance of the academic community. Whatever else seminary is, it is an opportunity to share in a community in which there is relative indifference to his ideological and moral behavior. (The fact that this may come as a surprise to seminary deans does not in the least temper its truth.) The interest-creating and interest-consuming institutions and the anonymity of the student allow him to pursue a variety of interests. The contrast of the seminary with the majority of the churches creates some significant problems for the life style of the minister.

From an atmosphere of excitement, anonymity, and intellectual stimulation, the minister moves to his first appointment or parish. His first ten years in the parish ministry are most often spent in rural or small-town churches. From the most urban community, the metropolitan area, and the most sophisticated institution, a major university, the young minister moves to the most conservative area, the small town or rural community, and into the most conservative institution, a local church. In a deep South conference of the Methodist Church, 71% of the ministers between 25 and 35 first served in places of less than 10,000 population.* Even if there is relatively little difference between the attitudes of rural and urban communities, there is a radical difference between the visibility of a student in a metropolitan area and the visibility of a minister in a small town!

*Methodism in the Alabama-West Florida Conference, Department of Research and Survey, Division of National Missions of the Board of Missions of the Methodist Church, 1960.

The curriculum of seminaries is not based on the role expectancy that the congregation has of the ministry, the role models of the clergy, or on any significant professional needs. Seminaries have almost no admission standards except a college diploma and a warm body. Several years ago one major seminary in the deep South admitted 175 of 176 applicants. Unlike schools of medicine and law, there are few persons with established reputations as ministers related to the seminaries. In fact, few things cause greater anxiety in a seminary than the presence of a successful minister. There is little dynamic relationship between the men in the profession and the men preparing the neophytes for the profession. Problems come when the young minister discovers that what he has been taught as the standard of a profession in a professional school is not in fact the standard at all in the profession and, further, that the Establishment is no more interested in his scholarly study of theology and the Bible than are the laymen who, according to Schroeder and Obenhaus, show "staunch resistance" to this study.*

Even though the standards of scholarship in seminaries are perhaps the lowest found in any profession, they nevertheless involve levels of analysis and awareness far beyond that desired, expected, or tolerated by the congregation.

The problem of role understanding is not resolved but intensified by the escalation of standards in the seminary. Though there has been a significant increase in the theological and scholarly training of the ministry, there has been little or no increase in the awareness of and demand for the theologically and scholarly trained minister in the

*W. Widick Schroeder and Victor Obenhaus, *Religion in American Culture* (New York: Free Press, 1964), p. 4.

Church. Moving out of a seminary in which the value system includes significant regard for scholarship into a church that has staunch resistance to scholarship is one of the first sources of role conflict for the clergy.

Another of the seminaries' contributions to the role problems of the minister deserves attention. The seminaries, almost without exception in the established denominations (with the notable exception being as always the Southern Baptist), hold a value system for the ministry that incorporates social action. The emphasis varies greatly from seminary to seminary, but the variation is in degree rather than in kind. More important, most seminaries encourage the ministerial student to assume a value system and a definition of his role that embrace social action. The attitude of the local congregation toward social action is most clearly seen in the fact that segregation in our society is most clearly achieved at the eleven o'clock hour of worship on Sunday. According to a Gallup poll, 60 percent of Protestants look unfavorably upon clergy becoming involved in civil rights issues and 71 percent consider the civil rights movement to be influenced by communists.*

Most successful ministers resolve the predicament the seminary has created by simply ignoring what they have learned in seminary or by assuming that the seminary is the best place to learn what not to do as a professional minister. Both of these postures, however, create new tensions for the clergy, for they are forced to learn new standard operational procedures without the benefit of instruction. It becomes apparent that seminary education is a dysfunctional experience for the parish minister and

*Hazel Erskin, "The Poles: Demonstration and Race Riot," *Public Opinion Quarterly*, XXXI (1967).

will continue to be so until the local church and the seminary have a more consistent role expectancy for the clergy.

6

Role Models for the Clergy

It is no accident that the most noted voices of the Church a generation ago were pastors of large congregations. The names Harry Emerson Fosdick, George Buttrich, Allen Knight Chalmers, and Joseph Sizoo are familiar to most clergy in established denominations as great preachers and ministers of large congregations. However, if one examines for a moment the voices of the Church that have demanded attention over the past ten years—Eugene Carson Blake, Billy Graham, Bishop James Pike, Martin Luther King, Bishop Gerald Kennedy, Dudley Ward, Robert Spike, Dave Wilkerson, and Norman Vincent Peale are among the most audible voices of the Church in our day—he finds that not one of them has been primarily the pastor of a congregation during the past twenty years. Dr. King, until his untimely death, served as pastor; however, no one could seriously argue that either the Dexter Avenue Baptist Church or the Ebenezer Baptist Church is a serious consideration in defining his impact upon the American Church. With the exception of Norman Vincent Peale, not one churchman who is pastor of a congregation in America can be considered a part of the national voice of the Church or the national image of the Church.

Some of the factors involved in the emergence of a new role model for the clergy can be seen by using Max Weber's concept of "ideal type," modifying it to "ideal event." By "ideal type" Weber refers to a process of abstraction by which certain characteristics are examined without assuming they limit the phenomenon which they characterize. By "ideal event" I mean to abstract from a complicated series of events those parts which can be used to enhance the possibility of a causal view in the historical process. The creation of the National Council of Churches (NCC) and, more important, the funding of a full-time professional staff for the Council have had an impact upon the concept of role and status among the clergy. Within each denomination, too, there have been structural changes that have influenced the role of the clergy. For example, in the early fifties every major denomination made significant increases in the funding of its denominational boards of social action. Social action ceased to be a voluntary action of each local church and minister and became a part of the total program of the Church. Programs on race, poverty, and peace became a part of the method by which denominations kept score on the faithfulness of the local clergyman. The NCC and the boards of the various denominations added additional impetus to the trend among the clergy to become involved in nontraditional roles. In the Methodist Church, for example, the General Conference under the leadership of the Board of Christian Social Concerns created an emergency relief fund to ensure pecuniary security to any pastor who became actively involved in civil rights. In addition to funding the role of dissent, the emergency relief funds became an additional form of status by giving the civil rights activists national contacts which could be interpreted as national status. The national boards reinforced the impact of the National Council on the historic role and status of the minister.

The staffs of the NCC and the national denominational boards quickly became the most visible portion of the clergy in American society. They also developed specialized skills and competence, while the parish minister found his role becoming increasingly generalized. The specialized skills brought to the parish minister a new sense of inadequacy which further affected his self-role. With the nonparish ministers dominating the visibility of the clergy, the role of the clergy suffered among its constituency, the local church. The presence of specialized skills and the funded roles among the NCC and denominational boards added to the clerical anxiety about self-role. Thus, the status of the clergy and his role were deflated by the clergy and by the parishioner, but for different reasons.

The second "ideal event" that helps in understanding the new breed of clergy is the historic Selma March, led by Dr. Martin Luther King in the spring of 1965. We must look at this event from the point of view of its impact upon the new role model of the clergy, of course, and not attempt to analyze its historic meaning for civil rights or for law and order. Dr. King issued a national call for the clergymen of America to join him in this historic march. Because the issue was drawn so clearly—at least in the minds of the clergy—by the confrontation between the mild-mannered pacifism of Dr. King and the arrogant cigar-chomping racism of the state troopers of Governor Wallace and Mr. Lingo, Selma and Montgomery became for several weeks the religious capital of America. Church groups from Boston to Los Angeles began to raise money to send representatives to participate in the Selma March. Seminary students and faculty also raised money to send participants. Numerous representatives of the NCC and boards and agencies of the denominations were present. The Selma March was the institutionalization of a great deal of latent sentiment among the clergy in the area of civil rights. In several ways it influenced the self-role and role models of many clergy. It acted as a reference group experience for many who came, and, with the passage of the 1965 Civil Rights Bill, it legitimated the goals and techniques of the clergy involved.

First, the function of the Selma March as a reference group must be considered. It brought together a significant number of clergy not only with each other but also with a number of authoritative figures in the profession. I had an informal breakfast in my home the morning the march reached Montgomery. Included were professors of New Testament from Southern Methodist University, of pastoral care from Drew University, and of theology from Harvard Divinity School, as well as board secretaries from several churches. Bishop John Wesley Lord's participation typified the involvement of the established church leadership. The Selma March, in short, was a value determinant for a significant number of American clergy.

Secondly, the clergy's sense of powerlessness was changed by the passage of the Civil Rights Act of 1965. The clergy found in the Selma March a goal that reflected their religious commitment; and, more important, they found a strategy that they interpreted as an alternative to the impotence they felt in the local church. The Civil Rights Bill of 1965 was interpreted, at least by a large number of the clergy, as the clear result of their involvement in the Selma March. Demonstrations became a significant alternative in the minds of many clergy to hopeless impotence in the face of powerful resistance to change.

A third result of the Selma March was the tremendous tension it created for the clergy who were accustomed to making conciliatory "both-and" decisions. Because the Selma March provided such a demanding "either-or" answer from the clergy, many who previously had subtly supported civil rights legislation came out publicly and emphatically in support of a role for the clergy to which there was strong lay resistance. The Selma March simply forced a decision upon local ministers and churches that they would not have found necessary to make otherwise. Being forced to make this decision affected the clergy's role and self-role most profoundly. I interviewed formally and informally most ministers of established churches in Montgomery following the Selma March. Among the clergy, I found, there was a significant sense of having been involved in a watershed decision concerning their concept of role.

The Selma March forced many clergy to make a choice which had a salient effect upon their preaching and the allocation of their time; it created a value-defining experience in which many participated actually or vicariously; it brought to one place and one event a number of status-shaping leaders who gave a sanction to a radically different kind of ministerial behavior; and finally, the march was related closely enough in the minds of the clergy to the 1965 Civil Rights Act to make the demonstration a significant form of strategy for the clergy. As an "ideal event" the Selma March was a causal factor in the emergence of new role models for the clergy.

7

Interest Level
of the Minister's Role

One of the most difficult problems for the minister to
accept or verbalize is that he is simply searching for some
level of identification and behavior consistent with his
expanding experience and values. Much of the anxiety of
the clergy and their involvement in a number of activities
which have low role toleration grows out of the fact that
much of their time is spent in activity that is boring.

Lay leaders, in reporting the complaints against the
clergy, frequently list failure to visit as one of the major
sources of dissatisfaction with the clergy. The traditional
role of the clergy, as any minister well knows, includes a
high priority on house-to-house visitation. House-to-
house visitation to some is an exciting part of their
ministry, but to others the demand seems almost primi-
tive. Many ministers seriously question whether the demand that they visit house to house is an important concern of the laity or a means of maintaining a menial job
definition for the ministry.

Some clergy seem to undertake visiting as a means of
role conformity rather than of real ministry. Ministers are
as aware of the congeniality syndrome by which they are

evaluated as are the sociologists. House-to-house visitation is one of the traditional ministerial functions which demonstrate clerical congeniality rather than competence or ministry. This fact does not mean that the clergy find ministry outside of the office unimportant. It simply means that traditional house-to-house visiting has become dysfunctional for a number of clergy. Even though many ministers visit house to house, this service functions as an indication that they are good Joes; to make more of it demands the hanging of great theological systems from textual hairs. The changing function of the home, the work schedules of parishioners, and distribution of members make pastoral calling a time-consuming activity with value only in the points it earns toward a high congeniality score.

The denominational meetings to which the minister is expected to go are studies in themselves. The phrase, "Mickey Mouse work," is frequently used by ministers to describe their attitude toward what happens at meetings which they attend. Perhaps the one clear function of denominational meetings is that of acting out status. However, in any meeting where a few act out their status, the rest must act out their lack of status. Meetings are often boring; and because they accentuate the drastic stratification of the clergy, they contain a latent divisiveness that is most disruptive.

Innocence is a gift of circumstance. Once it is gone, nothing short of mental illness can re-establish it. Having tasted the life styles of the academic community, the urban area, and the civil rights revolution, the clergy are simply unable to unlearn what they have learned. The need for filmstrip projectors and attention to the demands of Mr. Moneybags simply cannot demand the serious attention of many of the clergy once they have tasted the action.

We live in an action-oriented society. The Church is best symbolized by the little black and gold signs often seen on the doors of churches: "Open for Meditation." In a society that is open for action, an institution open for meditation is destined to create ambivalence among its clergy, who also belong to the action-oriented society.

We must remember that the great religious revivals of America were characterized as much by clergy finding different things to do as by any change in theology. In their day the field preaching of Wesley, the meetings of George Fox, the social service of William Booth, the camp meetings of Presbyterians and Methodists, and the revivals of the Baptists were all at least new things for the clergy to do when their traditional roles had ceased to exhaust their interest and time. The clergy of America are in a crucial period of change in which much that is traditional is to them boring, inadequate, or meaningless.

8

Battle Fatigue Among
the Clergy

One of the many tragedies of the changing role of the clergy is the price many men have paid in the trenches of the revolution. No amount of sociological data can meaningfully portray the personal agony and anxiety that accompany the role conflict of the clergy. Even the victims have had difficulty understanding when they have become casualties. Often one only knows they have fallen when he has stumbled over them in the dark.

In the ten-year period in which I have studied Methodism in Alabama, academically and existentially, I have become convinced that the constant tension among the clergy as their role undergoes change results in what may properly be called battle fatigue. Whether a minister is liberal or conservative, young or old, serving a large or a small parish, he faces an inordinate amount of tension. The effect of the tension cannot be measured by the statistics on heart attacks, nervous breakdowns, ulcers, or the large number of men changing professions, although statistics on all of these would make an impressive profile of the personal cost of being a minister during this period of role adjustment. Mental illness and psychosomatic disorders are so disruptive to the image of the minister that neither he nor the congregation will openly talk about problems of this nature as they relate to their church and minister. Many ministers go about their work suffering from anxiety and even mental illness long after those in most professions would have sought outside help.

Religion may or may not be a root cause of mental illness. But it appears to me that religion is one of the most effective means of hiding mental illness. Within the infinite variety of accepted American religions, the minister can operate with any mental illness that does not immobilize him. As long as he does not mention such issues as race or poverty and does not become involved openly with women, his performance is not evaluated by the traditional categories of sanity. It is amazing how much mental illness among the clergy passes for a new religious experience. The very vocation which creates the tension out of which grows a significant amount of mental illness provides at the same time one of the most effective places to operate while mentally ill. Several ministers who had been serving churches in the deep South during the civil rights revolution commented to me after they had moved out of the ministry or the South that they were sick and did not know their problem.

During the Watts riots, the Los Angeles police department discovered that officers left on duty more than four hours at a time in the maximum tension zones developed symptoms which indicated that they were unable to perform their duties with any objectivity. My contention is that in these days when the role of the minister is rapidly changing and when the Church is increasingly filled with tension, ministers develop emotional attitudes

that are similar to battle fatigue. Participants in the
changing role of the ministers are often victims of the
tensions present in the community and intensified in the
Church.

The inability of the clergy to handle constructively the
rising tension within and surrounding the Church grows
in part from economic factors operative in the Church
during the era of revolution. Because the average minister
does not have the financial resources for a vacation which
provides an opportunity for rest and recuperation, the
tension is accumulative in its impact and disruption. With
the possible exception of ministers in large churches with
multiple staffs, there is little possibility that a minister
will get the type and length of vacation needed. Even in
cases where a vacation is financially possible, the very
tension in the local church makes ministers reluctant to
take vacations. The minister's fear of allowing the church
to run itself reflects more than an inflated evaluation of
the minister's sense of importance. The very tension in
the church which creates the need for an extended vacation also continually demands the subtle hand of the
minister to keep it from getting out of control. In
churches where the minister is the only paid staff member and where the congregation is in constant rebellion
against the Establishment (and they are in many
churches), the minister seems correct when he contends
that there is more than one reason that he cannot afford
to be away. Methodist ministers in Alabama have taken a
week's vacation only to discover that in their absence the
official board of the church had met and voted to with-
draw from the parent denomination. Ministers in other
parts of the country have returned from vacations to
discover that the denominational literature had been removed from the church school. Others have had to face

the news that their church would no longer support the National Council of Churches.

When one considers the finances of the average clergyman and the constant diligence necessary to keep the average church committed to its program, the reason why few ministers have meaningful vacations becomes obvious. The absence of vacations is, however, only one reason for battle fatigue among clergy.

Another source of fatigue is the tension created within the family as it attempts to adjust to the finances accepted as adequate in the church. One minister's daughter expressed to me the dilemma in this manner: the minister lives on faith, his wife lives on hope, and his children live on charity! As the changing role of the ministry creates problems of inadequacy for the minister, the problem is complicated by a sense of inadequacy in his role as a husband and father.

The fatigue of the new breed is more than physical or psychological fatigue. One of the men has described it as soul fatigue. It is a fatigue which grows from the hopelessness one feels as he sees everything he believes in compromised or eliminated altogether in the life of the Church. In a letter one of the new breed, attempting to serve in a small black belt church, said, "I realize that the effort is futile. So what is my attitude now—one of utter hopelessness—despair. I am almost as low as a fellow can get and still keep his cool." Hopelessness has its own form of fatigue. Many of the men who have tried to serve in the deep South for the past fifteen years are soul tired. Their struggles with overt and subtle manifestations of racism have left them with a soul fatigue which is the most desperate form of despair.

The Establishment, for the most part, is totally unaware of the internal struggles men all about it face every

day simply trying to stay alive. The clergy in significant
numbers need professional care, extended rest, and—most
of all—a sense of hope and appreciation.

9

The Organization Man
Becomes Disorganized

No conflict in the ministry is more disruptive to many ministers than that created by the demands of the bureaucracy for legitimation, authority, and financial support. The bureaucracy has created a value system in the Church in which the bureaucracy's support is the primary measure of a minister's loyalty to the denomination, to its leadership, and to the emphasis they have invented which they call the Total Program of the Church. The congregation assumes that the most important characteristic of a good minister is congeniality, whereas the bureaucracy assumes the most important characteristic is the ability to raise money. More than one beleaguered minister has undoubtedly felt that the congregation calls him when they want the key to the rest room and the bishop calls when he wants the key to the treasure house, while he is under the illusion that he has the keys to the Kingdom. The increased demands of the bureaucracy for financial support have had several dysfunctional effects upon the role of the clergy.

One of the golden rules of church administration is that a man can work himself out of any problem except a

money problem. At the very time that the radical right
was attacking the NCC and the general boards of all the
churches, local churches were asked to raise as much as
twice the amount of money that they had raised previously. In order to raise the required funds, the local
minister either had to confront directly the numerous
attacks of the radical right—transmitted by local devotees
of Robert Welch, Carl McIntire, Major Bundy, Billy
James Hargis, Carl Prusner, and brothers of the cloth who
joined them—or he had to develop methods of subterfuge
to evade the issue. Both methods had serious conse-
quences for the local pastor. A direct confrontation with
the devotees of the radical right was most disruptive to
the image of the minister as a bearer of harmony and
congeniality. The methods of subterfuge became increasingly difficult for many clergy.

The methods of subterfuge used to raise money for the
NCC in local churches are symptomatic of the kinds of
conflict in which a number of clergy find themselves. In
the United Methodist Church the major request for funds
from the General Conference (the national church) and
the Annual Conference (the state-wide or area body) is
called the *asking*. (From the point of view of the local
pastor, the term means *demanding*.) The income from
this apportionment is divided in predetermined per-
centages by the Annual Conference between the General
Conference and the Annual Conference. A local church
cannot give directly to World Service or Conference Benevolence funds through the asking. The money that the
Annual Conference sends to the Commission on World
Service and Finance is then divided on a predetermined
percentage for the various boards and agencies of the
General Conference. The boards and agencies may give
money to the NCC by direct grant or may purchase

services as they see fit—without the approval of the local church that is giving the money, the Annual Conference that is apportioning the money, or the General Conference that is dividing the money.

Also included in the asking of each local United Methodist Church is an item labeled Interdenominational Cooperative Fund, the majority of which goes directly to the National Council of Churches and the World Council of Churches (WCC). Payments to the Interdenominational Cooperative Fund do not vary in the United Methodist Church except in the New England Area by region. As an example, the percentage of asking for this item raised in 1967 was approximately the same for the Alabama-West Florida Conference, the Nebraska Conference, and the Southern California-Arizona Conference. In 1968 the Montgomery District of the Alabama-West Florida Conference reported that twelve of forty-five churches paid something to the Interdenominational Cooperative Fund. Since the sum asked for is nominal, less than ten cents per member annually, one may assume that thirty-three of the forty-five churches refused to pay anything to the Interdenominational Cooperative Fund because of its relationship to the NCC and the WCC. In addition, of the twelve churches making payment to the Fund, only four had the item in the budget which was presented to the official board for adoption; the asking from the other eight churches was paid through private contributions. Forty-two of the forty-five churches paid a major share of their askings for the World Service and Conference Benevolence Budget. However, three times as much money goes annually to the NCC and the WCC from the money assigned the Commission on World Service than from that of the Interdenominational Cooperative Fund. The subterfuge is clearly indicated by the fact that even though 91 percent of the churches had either voted or assumed without a vote that they would pay nothing to the NCC or the WCC, 93 percent of the churches *did* pay money that went to the NCC.

How does this deceit happen? It happens because the ministers and church officials have agreed to remove the budget item which goes to the NCC directly, and they have then convinced the local church board that *only* the Interdenominational Cooperative Fund goes to the NCC. I have motions made by the pastors of local churches recommending that the NCC be removed from the church budget to avoid controversy; these motions proceed to identify the exclusive source of local support to the NCC as the Interdenominational Cooperative Fund. Some of the ministers who agreed to this arrangement were unaware of the deception. But in most cases the carefully informed evasion was a last resort to save the World Service and Conference Benevolence Budget. In many areas these measures were necessary. For some clergy, however, this kind of subterfuge borders on dishonesty and brings significant ambivalence to an already demythologized role. That such duplicity is practiced is one thing, but the fact that this kind of behavior is encouraged by the bureaucracy is another.

In short, the increased demands of the bureaucracy for funds and the legitimation of subterfuge to gain them have contributed to the anxiety of many of the clergy in the Church. Significantly, the Methodists for Church Renewal, the Black Methodists for Church Renewal, and numerous other grass-roots new breed groups have raised essentially the same questions about church finance.

A minister who is perplexed by the general role confusion of the ministry, inspired and moved by the clerical leadership in the civil rights movement, deeply troubled by the Church's lethargy, and disillusioned about the integrity of the methods necessary to fund the increasing bureaucracy faces problems of demanding magnitude.

10

The Birth of the
New Breed

The role of the clergy as perceived by the clergy, the Church, and the society has undergone continuous change in the history of the Church. The theology of the ministry has been as varied in the history of the Church as the life style of the clergy. At any point in the history of the Church we find a wide variety of understandings of the ministry, and it is risky to attempt to summarize in a few pages the development of the concept of the ministry in the Church. Yet there is some value in a simplified examination, which is not necessarily an oversimplification.

For the medieval Church, theology was the queen of the sciences, and the priest was the divine spokesman for God. Even the state bore the sword under the direction of the priest. In the thought of Thomas Aquinas, who dominates Roman Catholic theology even today, the greatest sin was error. Through the office of the Pope, the priest who remained obedient shared the authority of Christ in matters of faith and morals. Not only did the priesthood as a vocation carry authority and power; it carried a tightly knit legitimation.

54

Luther, with his emphasis upon justification by faith, radically revised the authority of the priest and replaced the authority of the Pope with a portion of the historic canon of the Church. The role of the clergy as understood by Luther underwent change. However, it was John Calvin and his followers who most clearly defined the role of the ministry as we know it in the Protestant West. Despite the pointed differences between the Roman Catholic concept of priestly authority and the Calvinist concept of clerical authority, the concept of the authority of the Church remained essentially the same; and the separation of the authority of the secular head of the state from that of the clergy was not clearly defined. The Anabaptists, the radical sectarians, the Separatists, the Quakers, and others who made the Act of Religious Toleration a political necessity introduced a congregational form of church government which had a radical effect upon the role and authority of the clergy. The movement from the priesthood of medieval Catholicism to the called and congregationally ordained clergy of the Baptists reflects a radical change in the role and function of the clergy.

The Church in America has seen the role of the clergy undergo three distinct changes. The Puritan preacher has been described as being invisible six days a week and invincible on the seventh. However, one has only to read the novels of Hawthorne to know that the authority of the clergy in colonial America was perceived in a variety of ways. The changing colonies soon replaced both the invisible and the invincible roles of the clergy. The revivals of the Great Awakening created a new role and a new role evaluation for the clergy. Following the Great Awakening with its emphasis upon conversion, the clergy ceased to be spokesmen for God and became public relations experts for the Master. As the frontier closed and familiarity tempered the gregariousness of the clergy, the authority and role of the clergy underwent a third major change.

With the conspicuous exceptions of Billy Sunday, Charles Finney, Bishop James Cannon, Sam Jones, and Billy Graham, the role of the clergy accepted by the clergy and its clientele following the Great Awakening has remained essentially the same in the traditional churches of America. Despite the profound effect of the social gospel movement upon the theology and the social conscience of the clergy and of men like Harry Emerson Fosdick upon their theology, there was little change in the clergy's role. From the conservative evangelism of Frank Norris in Texas to the urbane liberalism of Fosdick in New York, the role of the minister has remained essentially the same—preaching and counseling.

Following World War Two, the Church in America enjoyed unprecedented growth. From 1940 to 1960 there was a 50 percent increase in the portion of the U. S. population which belonged to a church. Church buildings arose at every crossroads. Church finances increased. Thousands flocked to the seminaries as candidates for the ministry. The Church enjoyed success in America as never before. William Whyte has described what was happening to the major institutions in America in a classic study, *The Organization Man.* Even the clergy were included in his description of the organization man. Out of the new affluence of the Church came an expanding bureaucracy which boldly thrust the Church into a new era of evangelism, ecumenism, and social action.

Billy Graham, praying first on the lawn of the White House in a powder blue suit and white shoes and then again in the ballrooms of the White House at the famed

Eisenhower Prayer Breakfasts in the shiny business suit
and Italian shoes of a Wall Street broker, was a symbol of
what was happening to the role of the clergy. The bouncy
optimism of the American Church was for a time not
inhibited by the expanding bureaucracy, the strange
voices brought home from German universities, or the
groaning pleas of black Americans. In 1953, *Life* featured
the ten outstanding preachers in America. The new President joined the Church on profession of faith, and Billy
Graham went to Boston. Almost unnoticed, a young
Negro clergyman walked the halls of Boston University
searching for more knowledge about Gandhi, Thoreau,
Brightman, and Jesus. A newly elected young congress-
man settled quietly in Washington.

The Church, like an embarrassed child, began to read
the *Reader's Digest* and discovered that Stanley High was
writing about "Methodism's Pink Fringe." It looked at its
seminaries and discovered that students were reading such
strange authors as Kierkegaard, Barth, Brunner, Tillich,
Niebuhr, Bonhoeffer, and Bultmann. The Church moved
quickly to bureaucratize its problems and make them
manageable. It withdrew its sanction from independent
social action groups and created new boards of social
concern. It organized new seminaries to intimidate the
old. The Church moved into the late fifties with a pervasive awareness that the radical right would not be
satisfied by mild statements of repudiation, nor would
the new emphasis upon social action be eliminated by the
bureaucracy. It reluctantly noted that the secularism recorded by Whyte would be a continuing influence in the
definition of the life style of America.

The increasing bureaucratic style of the institutional
Church, the intensified attacks of the radical right, the
irresistible commitment of black Americans and their

white allies to freedom and equality, and the prolifer-
ation of secularism were having a salient influence upon
the Church and its primary visible symbol, the clergy.
Out of the turbulent womb of the late fifties and the
early sixties was born a new breed of clergy. In a speech
on May 17, 1967, Carlyle Marney offered this description: "There is a new breed of holy-man. His name is
Legion for he is many. He is semi-holy, possessed, involved, secular, committed, realist, and revolutionary."*

The new breed of clergy are like the Priest Melchize-
dek: " ... He has no father, no mother, no lineage, his
years have no beginning ... " (Heb. 7:3). No common
theological background or position seems to characterize
the theology of the new breed. They have no single
denomination, and yet they are a part of all denominations. They vary widely in theology, style, and heritage
without a firm commitment to any theology, style, or
heritage. They are in many ways an expression of the
Church's refusal to become a victim of cultural shock.
The rise of the new breed, with their interest and commitment to a new role for the clergy, may be interpreted
as a significant source of the role conflict in the profession and, at the same time, a courageous attempt to
resolve that conflict. The new breed, though they have no
lineage, grow out of the turbulent decades since 1946,
when the Church began searching for adaptive techniques. The new breed are the historical, though not the
logical, response of men to the demands of consciences
created by a Church interested in social action but not
yet aware of the price.

*"The New Breed's Man" (Speech, Ministers and Missionaries
Benefit Board, American Baptist Convention, Pittsburgh, Pa.,
1967).

Some cogent reasons which are not necessarily related to doctrinal difficulties can be formulated to explain the appearance of the new breed. The emergence of a new breed is first the inevitable result of overtraining the minister for his role as viewed by his clientele. The minister in the typical parish finds no use for the significant scholarship and insight into social issues which dominate his theological education. The professional training of the minister would be a source of help and gratification only if there were some relationship between formal academic training and the role expectancy of the churches. The ministry as seen by the clientele and the Establishment is essentially a menial job, and like most menial jobs it becomes boring for persons who have greater than average experience or training. Many of the clergy who leave pastors' meetings for city hall do so from understandable boredom. The activities of the new breed are in part determined by their search for activity which in their value system has some meaning and interest. Only a young minister who has spent tension-filled afternoons in the islands of antiquity called small towns can know the utter desperation many overtrained clergy feel as they struggle hopelessly to be what they are by commitment and training. Pleasant as the long afternoon visits to the coffee shop are, they cannot satisfy the sense of mission stirred by the professional training of the seminary.

The birth of the new breed is essentially an attempt to reopen the question of identity for those who have made a premature identity foreclosure. Nothing in the experience of the minister-in-training prepares him for the fact that the profession is essentially a menial, impotent one. The new breed represents one way for the clergy to renegotiate their professional commitment. The new breed began to emerge when the role of the minister as defined by the congregation became obviously unacceptable to a number of the clergy and when the self-role of the seminary-trained clergy found little or no acceptance in the traditional parish.

The new breed emerged as adaptive techniques became necessary for clergy who found themselves in confrontation with the radical right. The constant vigilance of the radical right in attacking some ministers made it necessary either to change their style of preaching and involvement radically or to find other means of maintaining a livelihood. Personally, I know that no sense of impotency is quite so destructive as the choice of facing the radical right's demand for conformity to their ideas or facing financial boycott in the local church. As the political and religious influence of the right grew, some ministers were unwilling to accept the price demanded of them for peace. The new breed developed as a means of saying *No* emphatically to the radical right.

The loneliness of the struggle within the Church could be faced if there seemed to be any real purpose in the struggle. But many sensitive young men are no longer willing to die in order to do in the Church what was done in the Greyhound bus station in 1962. With their interest in power and even secular employment, the new breed of clergy have shed their cloak of sterility in order to combat the insidious devotees of the radical right, who have more influence over the local church than has any other institution of our society simply because the Establishment has decided that the Church needs money more than it needs anything else.

The new breed was created in part by the fact that "action is the name of the game" in our society. The only real action in the Church is crucifixion—usually the crucifixion of the clergyman who is interested in action. We must face the fact that the Church as it is presently structured in our society cannot demand the loyalty of people who are seriously interested in the struggles for brotherhood and peace in our day. The successful clergyman must not only give up any real involvement in the struggles of our day but must join the critics of those who would forge a new hope for brotherhood. Many men can accept the passive value system necessary to be a successful parish minister. Others, however, find that they cannot hide under a theological umbrella while a social hurricane goes on about them. From this group has emerged the new breed.

The new breed, foundering for a sense of cohesion and identity, found it first in the famed Selma March led by the archetype of the new breed, Dr. Martin Luther King. The concentration of the conscience of a nation upon one area of injustice gave many young ministers a new sense of power and purpose. Tangible results in the form of the 1965 Civil Rights Act helped to erase some of the self-doubt which plagued many of the ministers.

The problem for the new breed then became how to fund the role which they assumed confidently. The recent departure of a large number of clergy from the local parish ministry does not indicate disillusionment with the role of the minister but rather reflects their discovery of new means of funding their role. The new means of role funding solved problems for the new breed outside of the Church but created new problems for those remaining within the traditional framework.

The new breed of clergy are continually searching for resources to support what they believe is their role. Funding for a creative role is a hope of a large number of this new breed. Anyone acquainted with the Church is aware that whenever a job which may be filled by a minister outside the local church is created, the committee is deluged with applications and with hints that certain ministers would be willing to serve.

The perennial search for a funded role makes the bureaucracy appealing to a segment of the new breed of clergy. The staffs of the boards and agencies of the churches are more liberal than the local clergy for several reasons. The level of exasperation which forces many of the new breed to seek the various openings within the bureaucracy must be among the crucial factors that determine the relatively liberal position of the boards. The bureaucracy is attractive also because even the new breed of clergy have learned that those who control the mimeograph machines control the Church. The concern with, if not for, power makes a position near the decision-making center attractive to them.

The numerous agencies of social service created by the Great Society legislation seem also to be attractive to the new breed of clergy. From Maine to Oregon, the various agencies of the Office of Economic Opportunity, Headstart, and the Civil Rights Commission are staffed by ministers and former ministers. Conference journals reflect the whereabouts only of those ministers who continue to maintain orders; in them may be found the names of ministers appointed to positions with federal, state, and local agencies. Mental health programs, alcoholic rehabilitation agencies, and probation services are among the vocations which an increasing number of ministers have entered. On the other hand, the names of men who have made a complete change of vocation to get out of the ministry are not listed in the journals. These men, equal in number to the others, have gone into these professions because their self-role could no longer be funded in the Church, and they have found a funded role more consistent with their self-role.

Still others of the new breed of clergy have chosen tent-making, earning their bread by a vocation other than the ministry. The clergy who have undertaken secular professions as a source of livelihood are in many cases as dynamically related to the Church as ever. In interviews with several men who had made this adjustment, I found that they are more satisfied with the new arrangement than with the traditional ministry. Their sense of freedom and independence, in their judgment, has made them better servants of the Church. On one state college campus I found seven persons who had previously been in the ministry and turned to teaching in order to fund their self-role. All of the men were actively involved in the life of the local churches and were among those most willing to move toward the growing edge of the Church.

A final adaptive technique for financial support is that of multiple employment. With the addition of departments of religion to state colleges and universities, many ministers have found part-time employment as teachers. Others have accepted jobs as substitutes in public schools. In my study of Methodism in Alabama, I found various ministers of the new breed working part-time as carpenters, pecan salesmen, used car salesmen, marriage counselors (for established fees), stockbrokers, playground equipment salesmen, clerks in stores, tile and rug installers, athletic referees, hospital chaplains, golf professionals, draftsmen, and breeders of dogs.

The presence of the new breed will be felt in the Church for some time. The fact that they are not committed to a traditional ministry does not mean that they are not committed to the ministry of the Church as they understand it. The new breed will be grossly underrated if we do not understand their ministry as both an attempt to minister in their own ways and an attempt to create a Church in which they too may serve their highest dreams. We may hope that from the present conflict of role accentuated among the new breed will grow a much-needed understanding of a new ministry in which both the profession and the Church may find new life.

Since the Church is constantly pressed for money, and since few churches can pay an adequate living wage, the persistence of the new breed of clergy in pursuing new ways to fund their self-roles has been a significant contribution to the Church. We hear much about a shortage of ministers, but the statement needs clarification. There is not now, nor has there ever been in the major denominations, a shortage of clergy to serve the churches that can provide a living wage. There *is* a shortage of ministers to fill the small rural churches and the hopeless inner-city churches at salaries of less than $5000. If anything, there are too many ministers for the places available in which a minister can support his family. The new breed of clergy demonstrate a means of providing a radically different type of ministry without tapping the already meager resources of the Church. In addition, the adaptive techques of the new breed of clergy have furnished the often unimaginative church leaders with some ideas of how to provide the Church with a well-trained ministry in our increasingly complex world. The new breed of clergy may be profitably understood as a creative attempt to resolve the present role conflicts of the ministry.

11

The New Breed and the Traditional Church

Even though there is evidence that church members are most pleased with their ministers when they behave in traditional ways, even the ministers whom the laymen find most acceptable do not behave in what the laity understand to be traditional ways. What appears to be traditional behavior is based primarily upon the visibility of the minister's role. Most ministers have experienced a radical change in the low visibility areas of their role. Such disciplines as pastoral counseling, group work, use of audiovisual materials, and even sociology in the contemporary sense are recent additions to the curriculum of theology schools. As the major denominations have moved from sect type to church type, radical changes in the type of worship service and preaching have been introduced into the traditional churches. Most of these changes have been introduced into the Church with minimal conflict following the brief but tense controversy between the fundamentalists and modernists of the 1920's. Following the conflicts of the twenties, the major denominations did not become modernist; they simply ceased to be fundamentalist. The popular preachers of the 1950's and 1960's preached neither a liberal nor a conservative ideology. In fact, they seemed to ignore both. The preaching to which most of the laymen were exposed in large churches became primarily life-situation preaching, with a strong emphasis upon God's psychiatry and a limited emphasis upon theology, the Bible, and social issues. To characterize one means by which the clergy have adapted to the change in role as a new breed and to call another equally new mode of adaption traditionalist is unfair. Both that which is described as traditional and what we have called the new breed are new kinds of clergy, and perhaps the one is no farther from the traditional role of the clergy than the other. There are some significant reasons for laymen's low resistance to the adaptive techniques of what we call the traditional clergy and high resistance to the adaptive techniques of the so-called new breed of clergy.

The first reason has to do with visibility. The changes in the role of the traditional clergy have been primarily in areas with low visibility such as counseling, group work, and use of audiovisuals. The changes characteristic of the new breed of clergy, such as involvement through action and preaching in the civil rights revolution and the peace movement, have had high visibility. It is only with a good deal of effort that they have acquired this visibility.

The second reason the changes of the traditional clergy have been accepted with low resistance is the nature of the change. The role changes of the traditional clergy were primarily changes in how they did what they did, whereas the role changes among the new breed changed not only the way they operated but also that upon which they were operating. The traditional clergy were placing emphasis upon guilt resolution techniques such as counseling and psychological preaching, while the new breed of clergy, with their persistent proclamation of justice and identification with the dispossessed, were creating new guilt for the local church. The role changes assumed by the traditional clergy did not cut across any of the established economic or sociological prejudices of the Protestant community. But the role changes assumed by the new breed of clergy cut directly across the grain of the most obvious prejudice, race. Moreover, the manner of effecting the role changes—by demonstration and by identification with the demonstrator—were unacceptable to their clientele. In the deep South, I know of ministers who were forced to leave a church for saying in a sermon, "We should be thankful that the civil rights movement is led by a fine Christian like Martin Luther King."

The third major difference in acceptance has to do with the type of self-role each group of clergy found acceptable when the old role had become improbable or impossible. The new breed of clergy were primarily interested in finding a new role which they felt was relevant and consistent with their value systems, whereas the traditional clergy found the role created by the changing church meaningful and satisfactory. Perhaps neither exhausted the possibilities within the Church, but both showed the collective flexibility of the Church in facing the role conflicts inherent in the office.

Nevertheless, reconciliation between the traditional clergy and the new breed of clergy is sorely needed. Perhaps understanding each other is impossible, but some good will come if the whole Church understands both. Before there can be any significant reconciliation among the clergy, however, there must be some meaningful understanding among the new breed of clergy about their own problems and the problems they and the traditional clergy create and are victims of within the Church. This is no time for either party to insist upon acquiescence or recantation.

The new breed of clergy must understand and accept the fact that much of their hardship grows out of an inevitable sociological process accompanying the turbulent social change of the past ten years. Although in some cases the established clergy have joined the hounds at the heels of the new breed, the greatest source of difficulty has been not persecution but process. We must understand that the Church, like any other institution, cannot escape the existence of role expectancy among its clientele or self-role among its employees. The laity have not been able to move collectively from the ethic of pietism to the ethic of social action at a moment's notice. They are as much victims in the rapidly changing world as the new breed. However, the majority of laymen with whom and for whom the clergy work have a deep concern both for the Church and for the new breed of clergy. As the laymen become familiar with what the new breed are doing and why they are doing it, some will join the efforts that have merit and permanency.

Some of the new breed of clergy will say that there is not time, but I reply that our only tangible resource is time. Mutual distrust has arisen between the new breed and the laity because the new breed have come upon the scene exposing and defending a role for the clergy and the Church radically different from that in which the average layman developed his understanding of the Church and the ministry. Unless the new breed can fearlessly and fairly understand the dilemma they have created for the average layman, they will have failed in what I understand to be the spirit of the Lord. The new breed of clergy, let us remember, have no gnostic powers. If the ideals and roles which they bring to the Church have any merit, they can be learned and shared within the historic Christian community. Perhaps the new breed cannot or should not be the major expression of the Church to the world. The test of their fiber and faith will ultimately be whether or not they can become an expression of the way in which the Church relates to the world. They have proved that they are willing to be hurt for their faith, but that means little unless they can prove that the cause for which they were hurt is more important than the fact that they were hurt.

Since some of the new breed of clergy have become infatuated with such ideas as "the underground church" and "the church within the Church," a word concerning these terms is in order. For all people to become involved in groups in which they feel accepted and acceptable is mutually rewarding. The New Testament concept of the Church emphasizes the Church as a community and admonishes its people to be careful of the persons with whom they yoke themselves. Separation may be as legitimate a temporary strategy for the new breed as it was for the members of the early Church, for George Fox, or for John Wesley. Yet we must be acutely aware of the latent hypocrisy in such concepts as "the underground church" or "the church within the Church." There is the danger, in the words of Thomas Carlyle, of gazing at our navels. Ironically, a group that is most concerned about relating to the world finds basic reservations about relating to the Church. Many movements have gone underground thinking they were the true seeds of the Church, only to discover that their self-righteous attitudes made them compost piles.

The new breed must meet together so that they "are mutually encouraged by each other's faith." John and Charles Wesley discovered enough wrong in the Church to found the Holy Club; but Charles found in the home of a mechanic a faith that took him to the Church and the world. John found his power at somebody else's meeting in a small room on Aldersgate Street. What is wrong in the Church and the world is reason enough to call the new breed into holy clubs, but what is right in their hearts will send them into the world and the Church.

With a humility before God, they must not despair of their fate. The new breed has forced the Church to face the issues of poverty and race. If tomorrow the new breed disappear, the issues to which they called attention will forever be written on the conscience of the Church. The new breed have forged out of their own agony a new concept of the ministry. While many in the Church were willing, in the words of St. Bernard, "to clothe our churches with gold while children within the shadow of our steeples went naked," God has used the new breed of clergy to recall the Church to an awareness of its mission.

Dr. Harold DeWolf, recently retired Dean of Wesley Theological Seminary in Washington, was formerly Professor of Systematic Theology at the Boston University School of Theology. In his classes, students who were impatient with the Church's slow progress in race relations would frequently raise serious questions about their continued relationship to the Church. Dr. DeWolf would listen to the protest and then ask, "Where did you get your ideas about brotherhood and justice?" The students had to reply, "From the Church." Dr. DeWolf would reply, "So did I." The new breed of clergy must be accepted as a legitimate expression of the Christian Church and, in turn, must remember where they found the faith, the courage, and the vision that led them to create a new breed.

12

The New Breed and the Establishment

The words *establishment* and *bureaucracy* frequently appear in the protest jargon of our day within and outside the Church. Protest leaders among student groups make great use of the word *establishment*, which, their critics hasten to point out, is seldom defined. George Wallace received his second loudest cheers when he promised that if elected President in 1968 he would take the briefcases of all the bureaucrats and throw them into the Potomac.

The new breed of clergy share with other protest groups of the right and the left a disenchantment with what they too call the Establishment or bureaucracy. The historic separation within the Church in the West is due in part to the inability of the established leadership and the bureaucracy to manage tension without permitting separation. Clergy may leave the Church because of disenchantment with the laity, but new denominations and movements inevitably grow out of conflict with the Establishment and the bureaucracy. The Lutheran reformation, the Wesleyan revival, the Separatist revolt of Roger Williams, and the Society of Friends movement all grew out of the tension between the Establishment or bureaucracy and those who felt they had no voice.

Historically, the major denominations have developed around questions of legitimation. The determinative issues in Luther's "justification by faith," Wesley's doctrine of free grace, the Separatists' "baptism of believers," and the Pentecostal emphasis upon "gifts of the Spirit" all have to do with the rights of legitimation and thus the rights of dominance. The present conflict within the Roman Catholic Church in part is related to the right of legitimation. Underlying the birth control controversy is the more important issue of legitimating control. The present conflict in the Roman Catholic Church will not be resolved if the Pope changes his position on birth control, for this schism is a surface manifestation of the much deeper problem of conflict over the right of legitimation, for which the Pope assumes authority.

As the followers of Eugene McCarthy raised the question of the authority of the Establishment in the Democratic Party, as SDS raised the question of purpose in the academic community, as Wallace rallied his followers around the promise to revoke the guidelines, the new breed is raising the questions of authority, purpose, and legitimation within the Church. Unlike the McCarthy movement, SDS, and the Wallace movement, the new breed is not composed of students or of any particular regional group. Unlike the Democratic Party and the federal government, the Church has no resources to bribe or to coerce. The Church is occasionally able to punish its critics and reward its devotees, although the Establishment in the contemporary church has no real will to do either. Nevertheless, the Church and the new breed are moving on a collision course that will radically affect the established churches in America, unless one or both of the groups change significantly.

The basic questions raised for the Church by the new breed are in part political and in part theological. As in all social institutions, the struggle for power and positions among men and groups in the Church is constant. As in most institutions, a change in the political distribution of leadership makes little difference in the total institution. A trade magazine has remarked about the Presidency, "Presidents come and go, but the bureaucracy remains forever." Every generation of clergy includes its young Turks who organize and plan until they occupy the cherished positions in the Establishment, only to discover that another generation of young Turks is attempting to displace them. The struggles for political control of the positions of prestige and power are no more violent or more honorable than they have been for the past hundred years in the Church. The premise that all things begin in mysticism and end in politics is accepted within the Church. Most church leaders are equipped to deal with the time-honored struggles for power without undue rancor.

The established leadership of the Church had every reason to believe that the initial thrust of the new breed was a typical manifestation of the ancient and, in many ways, honorable struggle for power with the institution. The Establishment thought they knew the raison d'être of the new breed and made significant attempts to deal with them fairly. Young men were given positions of leadership and authority. Conferences for young ministers were for a few years in great abundance. Executive secretaries of boards and bishops openly praised the young men. If the aspirations of the new breed had been the traditional aspirations of the young Turks, one could

fairly say that the Establishment had acted wisely and
fairly in their dealings with them. However, the new
breed were neither young Turks nor a reform movement;
they were revolutionaries whose motive was not to get a
piece of the action but to eliminate the existing action.

The politics of the new breed was a logical and pre-
dictable expression of their theological training and commitment. For the past fifty years the Establishment of
the major denominations in America has been dominated
by the liberal theology of Albert Knudson, Reinhold
Niebuhr, Henry Nelson Wieman, Harry Emerson Fosdick,
and other devotees of evolution. The theological heroes
of the generation of which the established leaders are a
part were, by and large, thinkers who emphasized social
evolution, human personality, progressive revelation,
Sabellian Christology, and then died peacefully in bed
after a fifty-year career of teaching or preaching along the
eastern shore of America. After the struggles with the
fundamentalists during the twenties and thirties, the
Establishment settled down with a relatively liberal theology to implement the progressive evolution of the Church
and society. Following World War Two, a new mood
came into the seminaries under the banner of neoorthodoxy.

Neoorthodoxy and its crisis theology for a time dominated the theological scene. The Establishment rejected
neoorthodoxy, and not without reason. The Council of
Bishops of the Methodist Church in the mid-fifties issued
several statements expressly denouncing the pessimism of
neoorthodoxy. The language of neoorthodoxy sounded
too much like that of fundamentalism, which the Establishment had fought in the thirties. Neoorthodoxy soon
ceased to be a significant factor in the theological community. Its rapid ascent and descent were not without

impact upon the Church and the new breed, however. Neoorthodoxy raised serious objections to the theological sanctions placed upon progress and the legitimation of social gradualism. Its emphasis upon God as "wholly other" clearly demythologized the "tactical theology" of the Establishment. It called the attention of theology students to the scandal of the gospel. Despite criticism of neoorthodoxy by the liberals, it was functionally radical in that it challenged the progressive eschatology and epistemology of liberalism, which was the foundation for the managed witness of the established Church.

Whereas the theological heroes of the liberal establishment had been the happy warriors of liberalism who died honorably in bed, the heroes of the new breed were men who died in Nazi concentration camps like Bonhoeffer, were expelled from Germany like Tillich, were jailed in Alabama like Henry Sloane Coffin, marched in Mississippi like L. Harold DeWolf, were assassinated in Memphis like Martin Luther King. The new breed had a more radical theological education in which the ethical Jesus of Shirley Jackson Case became a Lord demanding radical obedience, as in Rudolf Bultmann's analysis. While the Establishment was proposing programs based on a theology of gradualism, a new generation of clergy were being educated in the tomes of Barth, Tillich, Bonhoeffer, Sartre, Camus, Kierkegaard, Bultmann, and Jaspers. For the new breed the theology of progressive revelation and ecclesiastical gradualism did not die; it simply never existed. Martin Luther King's emphasis upon Gandhi and Thoreau recalled a point of view that had been lost in the progressive theism of the Establishment. The new breed came into the ministry with a radically different theology which demythologized not only the modus operandi of the Establishment but also the legitimation upon which the American church had developed its far-ranging empire.

The real issue at stake in the confrontation of the Establishment and the new breed is a theological one which includes the basic question of the power of legitimation. The conflict is deeper than a generation gap and more profound than a struggle between siblings and the primeval father. It is a conflict that grows out of two radically different concepts of life and faith in the Church. The new breed has challenged more than the right of the Establishment to rule the Church; it has challenged the traditional basis for the legitimation of the work of the Church. The new breed, indeed, did not even pause to argue with the Establishment—perhaps the most conspicuous insult they could have shown. They simply operated as if the Establishment did not exist. The new breed marched at Selma, organized study groups for laymen in the thought of their theological heroes, went to work on college campuses, sought employment in the Office of Economic Opportunity, found ways to fund ecumenical institutes, and preached as if they had never heard of Nashville and New York. They did not leave the Church, as did many liberals in the twenties and thirties; instead they found new ways to be a part of the Church. The Establishment was able to handle them only as long as they considered the Church the only place they could fund their concept of the ministry. President Johnson's Great Society created opportunities for the new breed to move into jobs other than the local parish, an action which they have taken in great numbers; but (a crucial point for the future of the Church) they have not *left* the Church, and they still consider themselves ministers!

As an institution which in the past has had to deal with St. Francis, Peter Waldo, Martin Luther, George Fox,

Roger Williams, and John Wesley, the Church knows that the task of dealing with the new breed will not be an easy one. On the other hand, it must also understand that it is not a hopeless task. In the case of Bishop James Pike, Carlyle Marney, and the Rev. Joe Matthews, the Establishment has discovered that the methods for dealing with the new breed are not going to be easily learned. Yet I see real possibilities for the Establishment and the new breed to work together creatively within the context of mutual integrity.

In order to achieve cooperation, the Establishment and the new breed must recognize first of all that their radical differences are not going to disappear with a little more time or any cheap reconciliation. The answers to the deepest questions of the future of the Church in our society are beyond the immediate grasp of either the Establishment or the new breed. Both groups must understand their mutual desperation.

Second, the Establishment and the new breed must find administrative means by which they can live together. If the ordination of the ministry is to have meaning, it must have greater flexibility. The connectional church must find a form of ordination which connects the Church to the world. The historic provision that a man can maintain his orders in a connectional church only as long as he is in a local parish or in an institution under the control of the Church is inadequate to meet the demand for a ministry in the world. An order in the connectional church which permits one to minister beyond the narrow confines of institutions controlled by the Church would significantly reduce the excommunication of the new breed by the Church and, equally important, the excommunication of the Church by the new breed. Creation of such an order in the Church, which

would recognize the historical validity of the ministry of
the new breed without adding to the already excessive
load of funding pension systems, is both possible and
necessary if the collective witness of the Church is to
survive.

Third, the Establishment must carefully and prayerfully reconsider the historic methods by which all of its
ministers are compensated for their services. Churches of
the congregational type should set a realistic guaranteed
annual wage for ministers. Connectional churches can and
must adopt a plan of compensation which assures a more
equitable distribution of the total church income. Few
people consider the ministry an overpaid profession. The
highest-paid ministers and administrators actually earn
less than the average small-town lawyer or doctor. The
majority of ministers, even traditional ones, live in gen-
teel poverty by contemporary standards. Even though a
guaranteed annual wage for all ministers serving the
Church would probably distribute the poverty rather
than the wealth, there can be no real progress in the
morale of the clergy until the meager resources of the
Church are shared more equally.

Fourth, the Establishment must convince the new
breed that it is as interested in leading the Church as in
exploiting the Church. In a survey of Methodists in Alabama and West Florida, I included the following question: "Whom do you consider the most influential minister in the United States over the past ten years?" Of the
350 ministers replying, only 5 percent named a Methodist
or a member of the official establishment of any denomination. Ninety-five percent named Billy Graham or Martin Luther King, neither of whom may be properly considered part of the official establishment. The only member of an establishment group who was mentioned on

more than four questionnaires was Bishop Kennedy, and he had recently attempted to temper his position in the Establishment by returning to the parish ministry. The response to the questionnaire indicates above all else that the ministers do not look upon the Establishment as a source of significant leadership in the American church.

Fifth, the Establishment must reconsider the total system of values related to the definition of a successful ministry. Many feel that the Establishment already spends more money on bureaucratic programs than is necessary. The attacks upon the basically authoritarian manner of boards and agencies of the Church will not disappear entirely even if the Church uses its money wisely and spends the funds in programs other than bureaucratic maintenance. However, a radically different approach to program planning and funding will eliminate much of the resistance among the new breed.

Sixth, the new breed must recognize that contribution to the Christian witness is not exhausted by social concerns. The issue is not whether the Church does the current thing or the traditional thing. The issue is whether or not the Church is faithful to the total gospel for the total man. As the new breed find the freedom in Christ to do what they feel should be done, they must be cautious to allow the same freedom to men who by nature and training are more traditional in their approach to the ministry.

Seventh, racism in the Church must be dealt with where it is most conspicuous and where action will be most costly, in the local church. There is some integration and ecumenism at the top of the Church, but its presence there costs little. The Church, moreover, must be purified of the groups, values, and emotions that breed racism. A denomination might lose half its members if it began a meaningful attempt to confront the racism that is indigenous to the local church. Every Men's Bible Class in America might be closed. Yet the witness of the Church at the local level cannot be allowed to be dominated by latent racism. In the name of all that is holy, the Church cannot offer shelter to persons who represent the most significant vestige of racism in America, regardless of how much they mean to the Church otherwise. A serious attempt to make the Church an inclusive fellowship would rally men from every corner of our society to the ministry. As long as the Establishment is content to tolerate latent and actual racism in the Church, the new breed will grow; the Church will literally be emptied in the name of Christ.

There is a saying around Washington, "The right to be heard does not include the right to be taken seriously." The new breed demands not only to be heard but to be taken seriously. To be taken seriously will be costly to the Establishment, but the cost will not be nearly as great as was the cost to the new breed when they first took themselves seriously. To take the new breed seriously does not mean that the Establishment must accept their theology, their polity, and their action as the exclusive standard of the Church. It does mean, however, acceptance of the new breed as a legitimate Christian ministry.

The local parish system and the traditional parish ministry do not exhaust the many possibilities of ministry described in the New Testament, if indeed either is characteristic of the New Testament ministry. The Church has survived through the centuries because it has been forced to accept God's continuing witness in the Church and in church polity. With the exception of the polity of the Roman Catholic Church, which is feeling the impact of the new breed as no Protestant denomination is, no church polity has been in existence more than one-fourth of the life of the Church. The church polities of the Baptist, Presbyterian, Episcopal, Lutheran, and Methodist churches and the United Church of Christ have all been developed since the Reformation. The church school was added less than three hundred years ago; the Church had reached the ripe old age of 1,737 years before some new breed of clergy imposed it upon the Church.

The secularly oriented ministry of today's new breed is another manifestation of God's way to keep the Church alive and relevant for this day. Must the Church repeat the mistake of sending Wesley to his father's tomb, of sending William Booth out of the Church, of forcing Jonathan Edwards into teaching after twenty-five years in one church, of sending Emerson back to Concord? Or will the Establishment find the will, the sensitivity, the patience, and the courage to accept with seriousness the bright but sometimes confused, loving but sometimes mean, dedicated but sometimes antagonistic, heroic but sometimes vacillating ministry of the new breed? No one is wise enough to say, but there are many who pray that the Church does not have to be separated again in order for its sons to seek a church after their own hearts.

13

The New Breed and Race

At the height of the civil rights revolution, a group of students, black and white, gathered in Nashville to consider their future plans and strategy. A young Negro student proposed that the students attempt to attend the established churches in the city. The idea met with mixed reception from the rest of the students. The young man was asked to defend his strategy. He stood and quietly said, "People have every right to belong to a country club if they choose. All we can do is to give them a choice between a church that is a church and a country club that is called a church." Ten years later the choice of many of the churches in the South is all too apparent. Ironically, the only absolute segregation left in the South is in the country clubs that call themselves country clubs and in the country clubs that call themselves churches.

In the spring of 1959 a Negro leader in Bessemer, Alabama, was reading the Kansas City *Call*. In the paper he found a drawing of a young Negro with his hands held together by handcuffs and folded for prayer. The young Negro was offering this prayer, "Lord, help all Americans to see that You intended human beings everywhere to have the same rights." Attached to the young Negro's handcuffs was a tag with the following grievances listed:

> You can't enter here!
> You can't ride here!
> You can't play here!
> You can't study here!
> You can't eat here!
> You can't drink here!
> You can't work here!
> You can't worship here!

The Negro leader, Asbury Howard, had a large copy of the drawing made for the voter league hall. For this act he and his son were severely beaten by a white mob and sentenced to six months in jail.

As a result of the passage of the Civil Rights Acts of 1960, 1964, 1965, and 1968 and the heroic leadership of some famous and many unknown Americans, seven of the eight grievances attached to the handcuffs of the young Negro in the drawing can be checked off. Places to study, eat, drink, ride, play, enter, and work have long since been opened to the Negro by the cumbersome secular forces. In Bessemer and Birmingham ten years later, Asbury Howard and his many friends know that they still face the strange claim of the churches that they can't worship here.

Segregation in the South is limited primarily to the white man's golf and his God, both of which he pursues with limited skill on Sunday. This is not surprising, for in the past several years golf and God have served many of the same purposes for the white male in the South. Both golf and God are tension adjustment mechanisms that are vital to people as the level of anxiety rises. The tension among Southern males has risen geometrically while the tension-reducing mechanisms have disappeared or lost their usefulness. The new morality, which has been a source of tension management for much of America, has been of little help in the South because the Southern male has had the functional benefits of this new ideology for over a hundred years. The Southern male is essentially protecting what he considers his ability to survive amid the mounting tensions he faces as he loses his historic sense of dominance, his masculinity.

Golf and God are both means by which the Southern male handles his hostility and sublimates his aggression. Golf is a physical activity, but it is also an important myth system in that it serves several latent functions for the Southern male. God is a means by which the male handles his hostility, for his beliefs about God legitimate his hostility toward that which he cannot otherwise manage.

The doctrine of substitutionary atonement and its emphasis upon "the blood of the Lamb" must have an adequate psychological cause as well as an ideological justification in the Southern church. The religion of the Bible Belt is an adaptive technique for handling the primarily psychological problem of the male in the deep South—his diminishing role of dominance in his family, his region, and his nation. The doctrine of "justification by faith" is the ultimate expression of impotency in regard to man's ultimate destiny.

Furthermore, the preoccupation of the white male with law and order is basically a means of legitimating his own impotence. The vocabulary of the Southern politician is primarily the language of a betrayed maiden rather than that of a virile male ready for combat. A psychiatrist might make a profitable study of the use of such phrases as "crammed down our throats," "ravished the South," and "thrust upon us." That the most outspoken Southern member of the Senate spent his time combating pornography and courting a twenty-one-year-old bride illustrates the point most lucidly.

Golf and God for the Southern male are thus related to
institutions in which the male finds the minimum
threat—his Church and his country club. The Church and
country club are the two places where he feels safe from
such sources of humiliation as the Supreme Court, the
civil rights movement, and the increasing power of the
Negro. The Church and the country club are places where
he can act out his need for sublimation free from those
who have robbed him of what he has assumed—
mistakenly—to be his right of dominance.

Religion is not only a means by which people act out
reality, as Durkheim contends,* but is increasingly a
means by which people act out their fantasies. The
Southerner has found it difficult to force the Negro to
live by his fantasies, and he has found even more barriers
to acting out his fantasies now that the concrete society
based upon them has disappeared. The Black Muslim
needs the same isolation as the white racist if he is to act
out the fantasies which have become the substance of his
religious commitment. These fantasies can be acted out
only in private, because any conspicuous countervailing
fantasy would demand synoptic and critical attention
which the level of anxiety involved has no room for.

"You can't worship here!" preserves the anxiety-
reducing mechanism by which the Southern male has
accepted his emasculation without concerted, armed resistance. By maintaining absolute segregation in the
places where he gives attention to golf and God, the
Southern male prevents his most humiliating characteris-

*Emile Durkheim, *The Elementary Forms of the Religious Life,*
tr. Joseph Ward Swain (London: Allen and Unwin, 1954).

tic from exposure to the person he assumes is most responsible for the humiliation—the Negro, who refuses to be content with being dominated. The Church is the place where the male acts out his incomplete manhood and adds religious sanctions to the less-than-manly means he has chosen to sublimate his anxiety and frustration.

The Selma March made many impressions upon me which my understanding of history and social theory provided a basis for understanding. One impression, however, forced me to revise radically the analytical tools for understanding the South. I was unprepared for the myths which Southern men created and believed about sexual orgies in the Selma March. The closer the march came to Montgomery, the more intense became the preoccupation of the Southern male with sex in the march. He understood, perhaps better than any social scientist interpreting the events, that the Selma March would result in the emasculation of the Southern male in the Cradle of the Confederacy. Only the Southern male would interpret the song, "We Shall Overcome," to mean an orgasm of supererogation and would then behave as if his interpretation were fact.

The most desperate need of the Southern male is a sense of sexual maturity, a condition which seems unattainable if he is allowed to continue to enact his fantasies in the name of God and golf. Hodding Carter has referred to the South as an angry scar.* Ten years ago this might have been a meaningful analogy. However, the South is no longer an angry scar, for that term implies some masculinity. The South today is an infected scar, spreading its disease and stench upon a new generation primarily through the Church.

*Hodding Carter, The Angry Scar (Toronto: Doubleday, 1959).

The Church and the country club will be the last two institutions in which segregation thrives in the South for several reasons. These two organizations are among the few voluntary organizations to which Southerners have historically belonged. No civil laws or armed troops have attempted to desegregate these institutions. Most of the churches—with the notable exception of the Southern Baptist Church—have disciplinary prohibitions of segregation, but the national churches have no lawyers or police power to enforce their discipline. The only tool open to the total Church to eliminate segregation is moral persuasion, an inadequate tool in the deep South.

The churches remain segregated also because the civil rights movement has in most cases simply ignored the Church in its plans for desegregation. Although some attempts to desegregate the churches were made when civil rights organizations were active in Jackson, Birmingham, Selma, Albany, and Montgomery, they were usually minimal and of very short duration. The civil rights movement has confronted every segment of the racism of the South except that of the Church. If the Church were as devoid of influence as some think it is, this decision would perhaps be a wise one. However, the civil rights movement has failed to recognize that the myths of racism are created, intensified, and internalized in the Church. By allowing the Southerner to act out his fantasies privately, the civil rights movement has allowed the institutions in which the myths of racism are most dominant to remain essentially intact. Golf and God, which the civil rights movement considers least important in the matrix of institutions that it has attempted to change, are in fact the institutions the white Southerner considers most important. The Negro has aimed at destroying the manifestations of racism, and the white has placed his primary effort in preserving the legitimation of racism even if he could not preserve its most obvious manifestations.

The civil rights movement has failed to recognize that, regardless of how effectively one thinks he is dealing with its manifestations, racism will continue to be a dominant factor in the South as long as the agencies of myth innovation and legitimation remain intact. No civil rights revolution will have any permanent or effective value until the civil rights movement decides to disrupt, destroy, or penetrate the myth-making and legitimating agencies in the South, of which the Church is the most dominant. Taking away the privacy of the Southern white's attempt to act out his fantasies will do as much to eliminate racism as will any other single act.

The civil rights movement is already discovering—in the wide use that Richard Nixon made of Billy Graham in the 1968 election, for example—that the religious myth system is an important factor in the determination of the nation to resist the legitimate demands of the Negro. The churches will remain segregated because the civil rights movement has failed to recognize what every revolutionary movement must recognize: the revolution is never significant or secure until the myth systems embraced by its opponents are debunked or the institutions which generate these myths are radically changed. The most far-reaching social revolution of our day became possible with the recognition that " . . . the criticism of religion is the beginning of all criticism."*

There is a third reason why the Church will be the last stronghold of segregation in the South. Most liberals in

---

*Karl Marx, *Selected Writings in Sociology and Social Philosophy*, tr. T. B. Bottomore (New York: McGraw-Hill, 1964), p. 27.

the South—all twenty-six of them—assumed that even though the Church could not lead in the black struggle for equality, it could follow. They also supposed that when the motels, restaurants, schools, and Greyhound buses had been desegregated, the churches too could be desegregated. However, they discovered that the same factors which prevented the Church from leading the revolution also prevented it from following the revolution. The whites who applauded the beating of students who attempted to integrate restaurants in the late fifties, the flogging of ministers at the Greyhound bus stations, and the use of tear gas at the Edmund Pettus Bridge have finally found an institution in which their sentiments count and to which the civil rights movement and the Supreme Court have given little or no attention. The Church became the one place where a racist could go to escape the threats to his myth system.

The white liberals who helped keep demonstrations away from the churches in the false hope that the problem could be handled more effectively later by other means have helped an institution to continue its myth-making and legitimating function untouched by the civil rights revolution. The liberals who assumed that the Church could be changed by other means have by that assumption allowed the Church of the South to intensify its commitment to fantasies and to develop most ingenious myth systems, among them that of law and order, to reinforce their positions. Because the Church has had sufficient time to remove or destroy leaders sensitive to the civil rights revolution and to act out its fantasies without inhibitions, meaningful desegregation in the Church is less likely now than in 1958, if moral persuasion is the only device available.

The evolution of a new breed of clergy in the South is

in part a result of the minister's awareness that the
institution to which he has given his life in the hope that
it could lead is now the last stronghold of that which he
finds most repugnant—racism. The contradiction between
the message of the New Testament and racism is not
apparent to a significant number of laymen, but it is
increasingly apparent to the clergy who have shared
cross-cultural experiences and something of the national
political and religious posture.

The established leadership of the clergy poses a tor-
menting problem for the new breed of clergy in several
ways. A study of the social attitudes of Methodist ministers in Alabama showed that only 1 percent of the clergy
hold racist views, while fewer than 1 percent of the
Methodist churches in the same area have what is known
in the jargon of the Church as an open-door policy. Even
though the official leaders of the Church do not hold
racist views, they are quite willing to serve churches that
close their doors to Negroes. The ability of the established leadership of the Church to accept segregation in
the Church without serious questions contributes to the
growing separation of the new breed of clergy from the
traditional clergy. In churches with an appointive system
for assigning ministers to churches, the alienation is increasing because of an adaptive technique used by the
appointive authorities. Most of the churches in Alabama
either have a closed-door policy or are involved in an
internal struggle over a recently stated open-door policy.
Even though some churches in the Birmingham Area of
the Methodist Church either voted for open-door policies
or were informed that the policy of the Church prohib-
ited a closed-door policy as early as 1958, few churches
have an open-door policy today. The appointing officials
operate on the assumption that someone who gets along

with the people should succeed a liberal minister in a church. Therefore, a minister may work at great sacrifice and risk to achieve an open-door policy only to find himself removed from the church and replaced by someone who either opposes an open-door policy himself or will allow the laymen to reverse the policy. One minister I know served in a small-town church for five years and, at great cost to his career, maintained an open-door policy. He was succeeded by a minister who remarked on his second Sunday in the pulpit that he would shoot any nigger who tried to come in that church! The unwillingness of the leadership to attempt to maintain hard-earned progress in a local church contributes to the sense of hopelessness many of the new breed feel in the Church.

Granted, the Church is quick to condemn the poor racist who belongs to the Ku Klux Klan, but it is just as quick to elevate the rich racist to leadership. The subtle forms of racism apparent to the new breed of clergy are as distressing to them as the overt, unschooled racism of the poor. Yet the leadership of the Church seeks out the rich racist as if he were the Pearl of Great Price rather than a lost sheep. The new breed of clergy find the ambivalence of the Church in regard to race intolerable. Several have remarked to me as they were leaving the Church for jobs in OEO or Headstart that they felt the last place a person could be Christian about race is in the Church. All evidence indicates that they are correct.

The Church of the South, by maintaining its attitudes on race, is forcing sensitive men to leave the ministry. As long as all institutions in the South were segregated, a minister could convince himself that the Church was not as bad as the others. However, the desegregation of all major institutions except the Church and the country club destroyed that illusion. The minister is the only professional, with the exception of the professional golf-er, who is expected by his clientele to deal exclusively with the white community. A white doctor may minister to the medical needs of a black; a white lawyer may represent a black at the bar of justice; but woe to the white minister who attempts to meet the religious needs of a black. The new breed represent a vigorous protest against the parochial demands of a white church in a multicolored society.

The clergy are becoming increasingly aware that their presence in the Church contributes to the acting out of fantasies which are the seedbed of racism in our society. The decision to leave the ministry is for many of them a declaration of conscience that they must make to free themselves. A phrase that keeps coming up in interviews with men who have left the ministry of the local church is, "I feel clean inside." The compromises with racism necessary to survive in the Church have a psychological impact that makes sensitive clergy feel dirty inside. No theology of the Church, no desire for institutional reform, no ecstatic vision or charismatic leader, has done as much to create the new breed as has the latent racism of the Church and its acceptance and exploitation by the estab-lished leadership. This problem is not exclusively South-ern, to be sure. The director of research for the largest national Protestant church has recently noted that there is only one significant successfully integrated local church in America. The Church can no longer evade the fact that study after study has conclusively demonstrated that the highest levels of prejudice in our society are held by "religious people."* A layman who had held many

*T. W. Adorno et al., The Authoritarian Personality (New York: Harper, 1950).

positions of leadership in his church for twenty-five years recently remarked in an interview that he had never heard a minister of his church say flatly that segregation is wrong. The new breed of clergy in the South are willing not only to tell the Church that segregation is wrong but also to earn their bread wherever they can in order to preach brotherhood as a serious goal within the Church.

The resistance of the laity to an inclusive church, the willingness of the Establishment to exploit the rich racist, and the failure of the appointive powers to develop a clear strategy for dealing with racism in the Church have all contributed to the creation of a new breed. They are a collective *No,* in the ultimate sense in which Karl Barth used the term,* to the established leaders' compromises with the racist in an attempt to hold an institution of questionable value together through a social revolution. The new breed share with the black leadership a preoccupation with *now.*

The search for an inclusive church has made some significant progress. However, the new breed cannot overlook the anachronism of an institution which sets 1972 as the target for eliminating segregation in the annual conferences, when the Holiday Inns have been inclusive since 1964. The Church has neither the financial resources to bribe them nor the idealism to command their commitment. Theologically the new breed feel compelled to do what God calls them to do, not what the Church insists that they do. As more and more men find ways to fund their ministry other than through the local church, the conscience of secular institutions becomes quickened while the Church loses what meager conscience it has

*Karl Barth, *The Word of God and the Word of Man,* tr. Douglas Horton (New York: Harper, 1928).

had. The new breed represent a brain drain—they have the best academic training in the Church—and a personnel drain. But, most important for the future of the Church, they are a conscience drain.

The new breed will find a means of expressing and organizing themselves, and one need not fear for their survival without the Church. However, no one who loves the Church can help but fear for a church without the new breed. The established Church can continue to be a staid temple in which the ancient fantasies of primeval man are acted out. As the established Church's concern for the affluent gave birth to the Pentecostal movement, it will give birth to a new major force, the new breed of clergy. The established Church may save its manners and lose its morals; but the gospel of inclusiveness will be preached, if not in the Church, in the streets, if not by the established clergy, then by the new breed.

14

Adaptive Techniques of a Changing Profession

The ministry is a changing profession. The old role and much of its historical authority have passed away. Modern psychiatry has created a more scientific method for the cure of souls; the minister is therefore advised to send the complicated cases to someone more qualified. Bentz has shown that the better trained a minister is, the more likely he is to refer persons to other persons for help. He has also demonstrated that few agencies ever refer anyone to the minister.*

The emergence of modern welfare programs has made the occasional gifts of groceries and Thanksgiving baskets more difficult to defend as Christian service projects. The minister, along with the poor person, has discovered that the Church has neither the resources nor the will to meet the needs of the poor. The minister has lost no authority or power as a result of modern welfare programs, but he has lost the illusion that he could or should do something meaningful for the poor.

*W. Kenneth Bentz, "The Relationship Between Educational Background and the Referral Role of the Minister," *Journal of Sociology and Social Research,* LI, 206.

The minister has discovered that the historic authority vested in him as a proclaimer of the Word of God has disappeared. If the minister proclaims a liberal social gospel, he is quickly dismissed as too radical. If, on the other hand, he proclaims a fundamentalistic personal gospel, he finds the youth laughing at him while their parents assume that they could do as well as he does. The typical minister has learned to avoid both of these approaches and to bear down on life-situation preaching with all the aplomb of a stand-up comedian. If he limits life situations to doubt, anxiety, despair, and cynicism, at the same time avoiding hate, injustice, and poverty, he can also successfully avoid some threats to his self-image. However, he soon discovers that he has not gained status in the exchange, only toleration.

Those who predict that the ministry as a profession will pass out of existence as other agencies assume the historic role and authority of the ministry have not dealt with the resourcefulness of the clergy. As the authority-prophet-saint syndrome passes from the scene, ministers adopt other techniques to satisfy their needs for a role and for legitimation. They adjust by consciously and unconsciously choosing other syndromes to assume.

Phillips Brooks reminds us that the minister can never err in taking his task too seriously, but he often errs in taking himself too seriously. Perhaps the major professional foible of the minister is the passionate seriousness with which he takes himself. The minister who lives an unexamined life is constantly making subtle changes in his style and values, to which he is totally oblivious though they may be unbearably obvious to the casual observer. Because the minister has a serious responsibility, an objective look at himself is as difficult and painful a process for him as for any other human being.

Out of my own desperation to see what was happening to me, I devised a typology of syndromes which reflected some of my tendencies. Although I became vaguely aware of these inclinations in myself, I could see them with remarkable clarity in others. Perhaps in the descriptions following, admittedly exaggerated, others may see something of the subtle changes that can usurp one's energies in these days of relentless struggle for meaning.

The first syndrome characteristic of the minister is the *Dean Absurdus Syndrome.* This syndrome starts when a minister, finding himself with too little work, remembers a seminary course on the minister as teacher. After reviewing his old notes, he hears as impeccable a source as the assistant secretary of a general board solemnly claim that the Church needs ministers who are teachers. When the minister rushes up to the assistant secretary at the conclusion of his speech, he is disappointed at first to discover that the assistant secretary is talking not about an opening on his board but about what ought to be done in the local church. The minister, swallowing his initial disappointment, begins to think seriously of implementing in his church the program of education suggested by the assistant secretary of the general board. After much cogitation and some consultation with key people in the local church, the minister becomes Dean Absurdus. Dean Absurdus begins the tedious task of building his University of Relevance. Following the standard operational procedure to the letter, the new dean writes the executive secretary of the board of education, describing his idea for something creative and asking for help. A few days later a strange Volkswagen appears in the church parking lot loaded with leaflets, pamphlets, filmstrips, and golf clubs. The executive secretary has arrived to lay the cornerstone for the University of Relevance. The two move quickly into the office and close all of the doors. The executive secretary shares the latest gossip and the vocabulary he has just picked up at the terrific conference on poverty held at Miami Beach. Dean Absurdus describes his plans for a university that promotes real churchmanship, and he ends with a request that the "boys up there" might help. The executive secretary smiles and reminds Dean Absurdus that "they" are all involved in developing a multicolored brochure for the Adventure in Agape. At the suggestion of the executive secretary, the two rush off to play golf so as not to make the secretary's trip a complete waste of time.

Nonetheless, Dean Absurdus has discovered a good idea, and he will not be deterred by the inability of bureaucrats to understand the problems of the local church. He writes Dr. Carl Groupwork, his favorite seminary professor. A few days later he receives a packet of materials written just for a University of Relevance. The process now begins to produce some tangible results. Ads are placed in the bulletin. Notices go to the press. The announcements at the eleven o'clock service become vital and momentous: "Enroll now in the University of Relevance."

The most difficult syndrome for the clergy to adopt is the *Neuter Syndrome.* This requires that the minister find an outlet for his energy and interest that neither poses the threat of masculinity nor becomes totally identified with the feminine role. In this syndrome, the minister has neither the authority of a man nor the tenderness of a woman. He thus is able to remove himself from the conflicts of the male world without becoming involved in the more subtle conflict of the female world; he gives up both the power of the male role and the cunning of the female role.

If a minister in a revolutionary day can assume this syndrome, he avoids two difficult problems, those of threatening the men and exciting the women. But what is he to do with his time? He can become active in the PTA. No man feels he is in competition with the minister for leadership in the PTA; at the same time, no woman will identify his involvement as an act demonstrating virility. He may also take an interest in the aged without violating the boundaries of the Neuter Syndrome. This concern may develop into a full-time job. New homes for the aging are being built every day.

The *Raging Taurus Syndrome* is the most disruptive of the adaptive techniques which ministers may adopt, but it is unfortunately a common one. The social revolution of our day has influenced church members and local church officials to react to the minister in many different ways. If the minister is liberal, he frequently discovers that he must either remain silent or enter into a game of psychological warfare with foes who attack him at his most vulnerable points, his salary and the church budget. Church officials will boycott the budget and the worship services; they will attempt to hold the salary of the minister down because they claim he is not doing a good job. The minister is powerless to fight the weapons of money and rumor. He may make a valiant attempt to save the budget and attendance, combating the harsh boycotts with prophetic words and hard work, but the budget still goes down and attendance drops.

However the laymen may interpret their own conduct, the minister interprets it as an attempt to emasculate him. Whenever a male fails at his job in our society, he considers himself emasculated. As the laymen smile over what they have done to that smart liberal preacher, the minister begins his revenge. He bears his hurt in silence because he knows how to gain power commensurate with his needs for revenge. The minister now enters the Raging Taurus Syndrome. Having been masculine enough to instill confidence in the minds of women, he feels himself to be masculine enough to awaken the animal within them. Like a primeval tribesman, he begins to raid the village and take the often willing maidens. He proves his masculinity in a way that the church officials will never forget—with their women. Even though he most frequently does nothing concretely immoral, subtly and surely he excites the women.

When the minister enters the Raging Taurus Syndrome, the first thing he does is buy a uniform for his mission: a white turtleneck sweater, which he wears around the church during the week and for some pastoral calls. He is careful to wear it around women but never around men. He then begins to mention casually in the pulpit, without being judgmental of the men, that he is in favor of a single standard for men and women. This allusion is followed by a sermon in which he explores some traditional concepts of the meaning of being a man. As a text he selects the story of the woman taken in adultery, and he becomes her defender before men who would use her and try to get rid of her. By this time the women feel he really understands them and suggest to him that they would like to talk with him sometime. The minister begins to smile knowingly. The men interpret this gesture as acquiescence, but the knowing ladies understand it as a symbol of the Raging Taurus Syndrome.

In the average small to middle-sized church, the most effective syndrome the minister can assume is the *St. Francis Syndrome.* This syndrome gives the minister enormous benefit and almost no liability, and he is soon honored with the only impotent title that has some

47980

legitimation in the historic ministry: a "spiritual man." The St. Francis Syndrome has several advantages over other adaptive syndromes. First, it has many standard operational procedures. Almost weekly, new methods of prayer and of organizing of prayer groups appear. Conferences on prayer are going on in plush resort hotels with great regularity. What church will tolerate criticism of a minister for attending prayer conferences? Second, when the minister enters the St. Francis Syndrome, he discovers a group of laymen who are glad that he has had "The Experience." This affinity provides him with a ready-made group of defenders who have some voice in the church. Finally, in the St. Francis Syndrome he can talk about power and change with a minimum of resistance. He can deplore hatred, violence, and injustice as much as he likes, so long as he makes it clear that all of these should be changed by prayer. Although he begins to find himself washing his hands hourly, this new mannerism is a small price to pay for the assurance of professional security which he finds in the St. Francis Syndrome.

In the polarized society and Church of our day, the minister soon discovers that if he is to be accepted by his entire congregation, he must not allow himself to become clearly and openly labeled either liberal or conservative. For a while a minister may safely be identified as a conservative, but suddenly the liberals in the Church will demand equal representation. The minister has to make some adjustment in his image if he is to run a successful operation. His desire to please both liberal and conservative members forces him into the *Sand Crab Syndrome.* The sand crab is a tasty little morsel found near salt water. Its most notable achievement is its ability to move to the left or right equally quickly without being able to move forward or backward. The minister who enters the Sand Crab Syndrome is able on a moment's notice to move to the left or the right as circumstances demand. In this syndrome the minister has to be very careful about his sermons. He soon replaces theology with poetry, and his range of scholarship is exhausted by reading from different translations of the Bible. When he comments on any contemporary issue, he always adds a melodious, "On the other hand. . . ." The Sand Crab Syndrome seems to be particularly effective for persons desiring to be bishops.

Few people are willing to turn over to another person complete control of their lives. However, every church has enough emotionally weak people to occupy the major portion of a minister's time. In addition, almost every church member has some area of his life or position in the local church which he is most willing to turn over to an anxious minister searching for an ego-satisfying role. When a minister finds himself being consulted about the kind of drapes a family should put in their living room or meeting with the ladies to plan the menu for the youth banquet, he has entered the *Mother Superior Syndrome.*

The vocabulary of the minister in the Mother Superior Syndrome indicates the kind of total possessiveness that accompanies the syndrome. The minister constantly refers to the job as "my work," to the church as "my church," to the congregation as "my people," to the men of the church as "my men," to the income of the church as "my budget"; but he carefully changes pronouns and speaks of the women of the church as "our ladies."

In the Mother Superior Syndrome, the minister begins to think of the church building with the same sense of personal responsibility as an overly fastidious mother and housekeeper. The church building is not simply a useful tool to get the job done but a temple for the goddess of order and cleanliness. Pictures such as Sallman's "Head of Christ" appear in the church office and classrooms. Artificial plants line the vestibule and the ladies' parlor. The minister's concern for the building reaches a climax in his subtle recommendation that a small prayer chapel be added to the parsonage.

This syndrome becomes evident in the kinds of people who make daily pilgrimages to the church office. Having found a group of people willing to abdicate the total responsibility for their lives to him, the minister faithfully attempts to fulfill his new role. If one of "his people" fails to contact him, he calls "just to see how things are going." The management of a number of families is a time-consuming task and has all the external marks of a serious profession: the telephone is constantly ringing; everywhere the minister stops there is a call waiting to be returned; visits to distant cities become increasingly necessary. Some of those affected even consider buying a two-way radio set for their cars so the office can reach them more quickly.

Some of the clergy have higher ego needs than others and are more willing to adapt to a syndrome that carries with it status, power, and pecuniary reward. The minister with high ego needs, significant ability, and no worries about role conflict finds the *Babbitt Syndrome* most acceptable, for it has all the visible signs of prestige, power, status, and reward without the burden of any significant responsibility. The major liability of the syndrome is that it has high guilt potential for some clergy. The Babbitt Syndrome is characterized by its internal emphasis upon administration. The church becomes a beehive of activity, a large portion of which is devoted to "getting the budget up where it should be."

The posters on World Service are replaced with multi-colored posters with such slogans as "The Church is God's business," and "Don't give until it hurts—give until it is a joy." The tracts which the minister uses to carry the message in the Babbitt Syndrome are cards: country club memberships, air travel cards, a Rotary membership. It is amazing how many professional organizations and trade associations can find a place on the program for a minister "who understands our problems." This syndrome is one of the few adaptive techniques of the clergy that demands absolute withdrawal from the historic Christian community.

The minister is subject to a variety of external and internal pressures which have great impact upon his actual role without any serious effect upon his ideal role. Clergy have the strange gift of changing their behavior as ministers without changing their perception of their behavior. The adaptive techniques which ministers adopt are examples of what Paul Tillich calls "our remarkable ability to deceive ourselves about why we do what we do."

Conclusion

The ministry of the Church is many and yet it is one. The new breed of clergy represent one way in which God is working to bring a shattered world to obedience. It is not the only way, nor is it a new way. The traditional ministry represent another way in which God is working to bring a shattered world to obedience. It is not the only way, nor is it a new way.

The time has come for the established churches to cease contemplating the grandeur of their past and open their hearts to the substance of the faith. The time has come for the new breed to cease their praise of renewal and reform in order to seek collectively for obedience.

The continuity of the faith cannot be claimed by the established churches alone, nor can the new breed lay exclusive claim to the thrust of God in human history. The Church must find the faith to proclaim the ancient scandal of the gospel and at the same look forward with anticipation as God adds daily to the forms this proclamation must take, while it remains the same yesterday, today, and forever.

The established churches have long lost the authority to conduct heresy trials. More important, they have largely lost the will to ferret out dissent. The emerging ecumenical spirit of the twentieth century combined with the mutual desperation of the established churches has

taught the denominations in America one unforgettable
lesson: they are not one another's greatest enemies. In
the hard-earned and uneasy balance of the syndrome
called the ecumenical movement, *new* forms must emerge
within denominations as *common* forms have arisen
among denominations. As the new breed becomes an
institutionalized marginal group, it must internalize a
sense of relatedness to the historic Church and ministry.
As the established Church and its ministry seek to preserve the historic office of the ministry, it must remember that God has ordained the Church for his purposes
and must not think that the Church can ordain God for
its purposes. The traditional ministry and the new breed
can find in Christ a basis to be mutually encouraged by
each other's faith, rather than feel mutually threatened
by each other's faith. Those who feel they must *save* the
Church at any cost and those who feel they must reform
it at any cost could benefit from a God-sent case of
forgetfulness. The ultimate issue is neither to preserve the
historic forms of the Church nor to reform the Church.
The issue is a mutual call to obedience. Without this sense
of obedience, the new breed may create a deformed
rather than a reformed Church; conversely, the traditional clergy may leave a pickled rather than a pristine
Church.

There are several important reasons why the traditional
ministry and the new breed must in obedience to Christ
transcend the alienation present within the Christian fellowship. Both are called to a ministry of reconciliation.
Reconciliation becomes possible when through Christ
they learn that love does not keep score. The call for
reconciliation is not strategy nor polity but theology at
its core. Christ's command cannot be explained away by
the vocabulary of legitimation found in both the tradi-

tional clergy and the new breed. The message of reconciliation cannot become a meaningful proclamation of the
Church until it has become a meaningful realization within the Church. The ministry is called to reconciliation in
order that it may have a ministry of reconciliation.

A ministry that pauses to consider the appropriateness
of the gospel in a given situation has fallen prey to deadly
hubris. A ministry that does not pause to consider the
appropriateness of the kind of testimony in a given situation is simply not sensitive to the collective testimony of
the New Testament and the Church. The appropriateness
of the gospel in the human situation is defined by the
life, death, and resurrection experience of Christ in the
faith. The appropriateness of the form of testimony is
found only in the anxious search of the historic community of faith. The multiplicity of life styles in contemporary America does not preempt the need for faithful
proclamation of the gospel. Yet the ministry must recognize that differences in language, music, and art forms
within the American culture demand different forms of
testimony. The emergence of the new breed and the
presence of the traditional clergy provide an opportunity
for a collective witness which, if carried out in mutual
respect and love, is not fragmented but both whole and
holy. A varied ministry can provide the necessary input,
and the outcome is God's business. The new breed and
the traditional clergy perhaps both possess the appropriate message, the gospel, but they apparently possess
styles that are appropriate for different situations. In the
reconciliation of Christ, all can rejoice in this diversity.

The new breed of clergy must depend upon the Church
in its traditional form for resources to sustain them
emotionally, theologically, and in many cases economi-
cally. The historic counsel of the Church in scholarship,

biblical studies, and theology is a legacy upon which the new breed seems destined to depend. Yet the fire and passion the new breed has brought to the Church in its theology of confrontation, put into practice in civil rights and peace demonstrations, has caused the entire Church to ask searching questions about its obedience. The experiences of both the new breed and the traditional clergy are legitimate resources for the testimony of the Church. The hurt, loneliness, and despair which seem to dominate the consciousness of some of the new breed are not new to the ministry. Mutual understanding can provide not only collective resources of testimony but also mutual comfort and hope for those of both perspectives.

The new breed and traditional clergy have had different experiences as they have attempted to proclaim the gospel, but they have also shared common experiences. Death, birth, marriage, fear, hurt, anxiety, and despair are common experiences of men. In the turbulent days in which we live, all clergy share the rising tension, anxiety, despair, and frustration that accompany a changing profession. The need for the mutual support that ministers can bring to one another is strikingly apparent to those who have been forced to drink from a broken cup. A ministry to one another is one of the great possibilities for the traditional and new breed clergy—a collective ministry coming from a collective experience. In the great mystery called the Christian Church, few are wise enough fully to understand its past and none are wise enough to predict its future. Yet, soft-voiced priest and fiery prophet alike, God has called each to bear witness to the faith in Jesus Christ our Savior and Lord.

DATE DUE

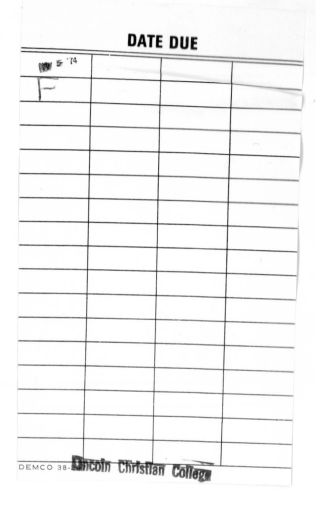

NOV 5 '74			

Date Due

JAN 21 '75			
JAN 13 '76			
Feb 13			
FEB 18 '77			
~~ '78			
OCT 3 '78			
NOV 28 '78			
JAN 29 '79			
MAR 24 '82			
SEP 22 '82			
Dec 15			